Project Success Stories

Real World Adventures in Project Management

Bill Flury

ISBN-13: 978-1985025097

ISBN-10: 1985025094

ACKNOWLEDGEMENTS

Thanks to all my friends and colleagues who have encouraged and enabled me to share stories from the many, wonderful projects on which I have been privileged to work. Thanks to Chris Fristad for his encouragement to produce this compilation of stories and his constructive comments through the years as I have been writing them.

Special thanks to Vicki Wrona for inviting me into her blog at ForwardMomentum.net and for publishing the initial versions of these stories. Vicki's top-notch editorial team: Ray Robinson, Cheri Milford, and Natasha Egan have added graphics and arranged and presented the stories very well in the blog.

Diana Fraser provided essential design and editing advice. The illustrations were produced with the aid of software applications by Wordle.com and Caricature Software.

Special thanks to Mary Flury who has patiently supported me in so many ways throughout our many years together and especially through the gestation of this product.

.

CreateSpace Independent Publishing Platform

Cover Photo: Created by Pressfoto - Freepik.com

==================================

A good story is often the best way to convey meaningful knowledge.

L. T. Davenport
Developing Organizational Memory Through Learning
Organizational Learning, Autumn 1998

==================================

Foreword

Learning to Succeed

Learning how to achieve success as a project manager can be difficult. Many experts and organizations have published tomes of recommended, standard practices and procedures one should follow to help ensure success. However, every project is unique, and the standard practices don't always fit the situations that arise.

Learning Through Stories

In 1998, Alexander Laufer and Edward Hoffman conceived a new way to help current and future project managers learn how to become successful. They sought out successful project managers and asked them to tell stories about their projects. They collected these and published them in a book titled *"Project Management Success Stories."* Their book contains 70 stories by 38 different project managers.

Hoffman had this to say about the book: *"Stories stimulate curiosity. People will seldom read procedure manuals, but most will eagerly devour short stories, even off the job. Stories are memorable. The messages stemming from a particular experience tend to stick and can be easily recalled."*

About Their Stories

Their stories bring to life the many ways that the theoretical principles from the procedure manuals can be effectively and successfully applied. The situations described in the stories are real. The projects from which these stories come have all been successfully accomplished, not by theoretical people in the assumed situations in the procedure manuals. but by real people in real-life situations,

The book has been very well received and is still a top seller. The stories are short, usually just a couple of pages. Readers who are currently working as project managers frequently find stories that relate situations like their own. Some read the stories to learn about situations they may face in the future.

Using the Stories

In their book, Laufer and Hoffman relate the story of one project manager who used it by reading one story each evening before he went to bed. About that, he said: ***"Each morning when I got up I could not stop thinking about the previous night's story. I kept thinking about it as if it was an ongoing movie. Whenever I finished a story I added another milestone on my road to success."***

That reader provided evidence that each story offers one or more special insights that you can weave into your understanding of how to make projects successful in real-life situations.

This Book

In this book, you will find 28 stories drawn from the author's experience in successfully managing 85 challenging and widely varied projects. The stories all relate to situations that required thoughtful application of the standard practices described in the several different project management handbooks on his bookshelf.

ForwardMomentum.net

All of these stories were published over the past three years in an exceptional on-line blog published by Forward Momentum, LLC. Each month, that blog presents a collection of new stories by several of their more than thirty contributors on a variety of topics related to their successful projects and process improvement activities. The Forward Momentum archive contains more than 365 stories from the past three years, enough to provide bed-time reading for a whole year.

Story Sequence

The stories in this book originally appeared in random order (i.e., as they were remembered by the author). Here, you will see that they are presented in the sequence in which projects come into being, pass through various phases and, arrive at a successful conclusion.

So, now it's time to start reading the stories…………….

……and learning about some of the ways those traditional "Rules for Success" can be applied in the real world in which you work.

==

"Stories create community, enable us to see through the eyes of other people, and open us to the claims of others."

Peter Forbes

==

CONTENTS

CONTENTS (CONCLUDED)

=======================================

"Stories tell us what we already knew and forgot, and remind us of what we haven't yet imagined."

Anne L. Watson

=======================================

Section 1 - Planning

This first section includes stories related to initiating a new project. You will have a chance meet some people from our successful projects and see what they do to help ensure that our projects succeed.

Evaluating New Ideas *- In the first story, you will meet Beth, a dynamic business development person for our organization. Beth's job is to find new business that will be good for us and our clients. Beth hears a lot of ideas for new business but knows from experience that only some will be good ideas for us to pursue. In this story you will see how we all work together to sort out and follow up on the good ideas and reject the bad ones.*

Getting Engaged

Personal relationships and business relationships. both include elements of respect, trust, tolerance, and tenacity. This story provides an example of the way a business relationship matured from "first date" to "engagement", and maybe more.

Planning by Checklist *- In the next story you will meet Paul. He is the person we have relied on to make sure that we know about and have documented absolutely everything we have agreed to do on our projects. Paul is a checklist fan and you will see why we chose him for this job.*

Specification Fleas *- Arvid is the star of our next story. Arvid has been on many projects over the years and has seen the different kinds of errors that people can make. He has seen all the product and project flaws that can make projects fail to succeed. Arvid jokingly calls flaws "Fleas." This story tells you why he does that.*

A Piece of Cake - The fifth story is about a young team that eagerly jumped into each new project without doing much planning. They quickly found out what it takes to make a project a "Piece of Cake."

Yesterday Today, Tomorrow

Each day on a project ends with some of the required work done and some still to be done before completion. Each morning, successful project managers adjust their plans to ensure that <u>all</u> the work will be completed by the target date. Re-planning is a constant. This story presents an example of the continuous planning and re-planning process works.

Plan B Was Yesterday

Enjoy this poem that can serve as a reminder of the need for continuous project planning and re-planning as the work environment and requirements change.

=================================

These stories can help you:

- *Select projects most likely to be successful for you and your clients*
- *Find ways to enhance your relationships with your clients*
- *Make sure you know everything you have to do (so you can check it off when you are done)*
- *Make sure you have found all the project "fleas" that can bite you.*
- *Avoid underestimating projects that just look "easy."*
- *Remember how important constant re-planning is to eventual success.*

======================================

====================================

"The story-making process enables us to simplify complex information into the core essence of understanding."

Y. Gabriel, Storytelling in Organizations

====================================

A New Idea

Evaluating New Ideas

A New Idea Arrives

Beth hurries into her team lead's office all excited. She's just come back from visiting Roger, her number one favorite client. She tells him that Roger has a great idea for a new App for his customer Service Group. The idea involves capturing incoming phone call area codes and matching them with certain census data to generate more information about the people who call in for customer service.

Beth says that Roger apparently had heard about one of his competitors doing this and wants us to get on it right away. It sounds like a good idea, but is it really? How can they tell? How do you figure out if a new idea will be a good project for you?

A Process for Evaluating New Ideas

If your organization has documented the process for evaluating new ideas, you would start by working through that process. If your organization has never agreed on an approach and documented an idea evaluation process you have a problem. You have to figure out an evaluation process on your own and hope that it will work.

Beth and her team lead have a process for evaluating new ideas. They follow that process for all new ideas – and the process works. Only ideas that will lead to good projects make it through their screening process. They have a great success record. Maybe it would be helpful for you to read on and see how their process works and take notes.

Step One in the Process: Collect Basic Information

Beth's process calls for the orderly collection of certain information about the new idea. Over the next few days (or sooner if it is urgent) she will do what is called for and will complete the checklist provided on the New Idea – Basic Info Checklist Card. When she has finished this she will meet with her team lead again to discuss what she has found out.

```
================================================
```
New Idea – Basic Info Checklist Card

- ☐ I have discussed the idea with the originator.
- ☐ I have discussed it with our experts and listed the issues they raised.
- ☐ I can identify a champion and all others involved.
- ☐ I have identified the final, tangible product(s).
- ☐ I have identified some risks.
- ☐ I have prepared an initial estimate of the effort required.

```
================================================
```

- ☐ I'm not convinced it's worth doing
- ☐ I think we need more information
- ☐ I think it's worth doing.

```
================================================
```

I have written all this in a Draft. _____ Initials

```
================================================
```

When Beth has done her homework and checked off all these items she will meet with her team lead to review what she has found out. If they decide not to proceed, Beth and her team lead will go back together to visit their client, Roger, and explain their thinking. They will discuss their issues and concerns with Roger. They will jointly decide to continue onward, resolve some open issues and meet again, or drop the idea.

If they agree to go ahead, they will take the next step in the process. The team lead will ask some of the team members with special skills to help Beth work through a second checklist. The second checklist reminds them of the things they need to consider about the feasibility of successfully realizing the benefits of the idea.

Step Two in the Process: Consider Project Feasibility

In the second step in the New Idea evaluation process the team members bring their specialties to bear to generate the information required to estimate the feasibility of successfully executing the idea. They start with the information collected in the first step and minutes of the discussions during the first step review. This is definitely a team effort and all the results are shared among all the team members.

The team lead makes one person responsible for leading the effort and completing and initialing the checklist.

==

New Idea- Feasibility Checklist

- ☐ We have read the results of the First Step Review.
- ☐ We understand the operational context (i.e., where and under what conditions the idea will be implemented).
- ☐ We can conceive of at least two possible ways to implement the idea and can explain the differences involved.
- ☐ [Optional] We have developed a demonstration model and can describe how it was used and demonstrated, and the substance of the reviewers' comments.
- ☐ We have identified the basic types of intermediate work and products that would be required to produce the final product.
- ☐ We have identified and listed the types of skills required to implement the idea.
- ☐ We have determined that the required skills are available to us.
- ☐ We have identified and documented the apparent risks
- ☐ We have documented our assumptions and made a rough estimate of the effort and time required to implement the idea.
- ☐ We can describe how you could demonstrate to the user that the product of this effort will fully satisfy the requirement.

==

- ☐ We are not convinced it's worth doing
- ☐ We think we need more information
- ☐ We think it's worth doing.

==

I have written all this in a Draft. _____ Initials

==

Time to Decide

When the second checklist is completed the team lead will have the information needed to decide if this is a good project idea – or is it one that just sounded good when we first heard it but should be buried along with many others that really aren't.

These two checklists and this process can help you determine if the proposed new project is:

1) Appropriate and sound? and

2) One we can implement it successfully?

==

p.s. After going through both checklists, Beth and her team concluded that they should pass on this opportunity. They concluded that they did not have the requisite skills to do this well.

==

==

Do you have a process to help you weigh the potential of your proposed projects?

Is your process documented, and followed?

==

Getting Engaged

The Announcement

Beth and Gregory came back into the office very excited. They called everyone together in the conference room to make a very important announcement. Beth broke the news: "We're engaged!" Everyone was thrilled, but not for Beth and Gregory who had sealed the deal, but for everyone, because this was great news for our company. Let me explain.

Body Shopping

Our company is like many new startups that began with a few ideas for some consumer electronic products we could make and sell. We have done well with our first few products and are always looking for ways to grow the company.

A few months ago, we had a call from a Widget Corp. VP asking for some help. She knew that we built similar products. She asked if we had any qualified production people we could provide to help them for several weeks with the software testing and assembly of their newest hot product. We would be paid for their time and they would work under Widget's direction.

Widget was producing an in-home, electronic personal assistant they were marketing under the trade name "*Jeeves*." They had received more advance orders that they had expected and needed to speed up their production schedule by adding some outside help.

We had some staff who were awaiting some new work, so we arranged to "body shop" them over to Widget. We sent Beth and Gregory and three others over to Widget. It was a good deal for them and us.

Becoming a Vendor

After three weeks of working at Widget, Beth stopped back at the office to share a marketing idea she had. She described what she and the others were doing for Widget. She also described the product and told us that *Jeeves* was very popular, and Widget was continuing to have trouble meeting demand. She said that we could probably set up a process that could make that product better, faster and cheaper and the client might like to have us do that for them. She suggested that we contact the Widget VP for Production.

I spoke to the VP and described our production capabilities. I offered to work with him to see if we could manufacture and supply *Jeeves* at a fixed price that would be lower than what it was now costing him. After some discussion between the two of us and some joint planning by their engineering team and ours, they agreed to a purchase agreement. We would take over all Jeeves production and promise to deliver as many as they could sell. They would be able to use their production line to start making a new product that they had designed but had not had the resources to put into production. As before, it was a good deal for them and us.

We Became a Vendor

Our relationship with Widget was beginning to grow. In the beginning, we were just selling them staff hours. Now, as a result of Beth's entrepreneurial thinking, we would be selling them a product priced such that both we and Widget could make a profit and we would also be helping them to satisfy the rapidly increasing demand for *Jeeves*.

Becoming Engaged

As we worked together, we found out how the client often combined *Jeeves* with its other products. We also had the opportunity to acquaint Widget management with our products and the similar types of work that we were doing. That's what, ultimately, led to the engagement.

Beth and Gregory had been working on the Widget contract from the outset. They started with the hourly group and stayed with it while we set up our *Jeeves* production line. They sat in on all the discussions of how we might start to integrate our products and production lines with Widget's. They were the leaders in bringing our two companies together. Today was the day they had gone to see the Widget VP about establishing a new, closer relationship -- an engagement -- a promise to work together on many new ventures of mutual interest.

No Surprise

You may have been puzzled by the fact that the excitement about the "We're engaged!" announcement was not about Beth and Gregory. Everyone there knew that Beth and Gregory were both happily married to their respective spouses. The real excitement was about the new, closer relationship between our company and Widget. That was good news for everyone because it would provide more new, exciting and rewarding work for everyone.

How Personal Relationships Develop

- Two people meet.
- They spend some time together.
- They get to know each other, what they can do, what they like to do.
- They find some things to do together.
- They do more of those things and enjoy doing them together.
- They get "engaged" and plan for a wonderful future.

That's how it works for people. Can businesses do the same?

Our Path to the Engagement

Beth and Gregory were both imbued with the entrepreneurial spirit of our company. As they worked with Widget, they followed the same path that people do to develop their relationships. Their marketing strategy and activities played out well. Our two companies are now engaged and working and planning together for a wonderful future.

Two companies, with similar product lines and markets, similarly qualified staff, working together successfully -- Could marriage be in the offing?

==

Planning by Checklist

Learning Paul's Secret

Several people told me I had to meet and talk with Paul. Paul is an exceptional project manager in a government contractor organization. In the past eight years he has successfully run many projects, all of which have been on time, on budget, and highly praised by his clients. I was happy to catch up with him and get time for him to tell me how he was able to do so well.

Paul told me that his secret was to use checklists. He said that he was inspired to use them after he read the Checklist Manifesto by Atul Gawande. After reading that and thinking about his projects he saw how they could work for him and developed a set of checklists that would help him ensure that he would surface and address all the important aspects of his projects from start to finish.

How Checklists Helped Paul

It was surprising to hear all the different ways that he found checklists to be useful. He told me he used them for:

- Determining Project Scope
- Ensuring complete requirements collection
- Controlling requirements changes
- Prioritizing tasks
- Delegating tasks
- Making sure everything on his projects was done before final delivery

As he explained it, he was using his checklists in stages throughout each project to make sure he was seeing everything he needed to see along the way so that he would understand what he had to be doing at any point in the process.

Checklists Through the Project Cycle

Paul went through the whole project cycle with me and explained how he was using some of his checklists.

Project Start Up

At the beginning of each project he would sit down with his project team and they would discuss what the project was supposed to accomplish. Then they would use their Stakeholder Checklist to help them list all the people that might be involved in the project and note how they might be involved.

The Stakeholder Checklist was one that Paul had built over the years. His original version was based on a generic one that his professional association had developed over the past few years. It contained the wisdom accumulated from many projects and expert project managers. Paul maintained the checklist as a "living" document. Every time Paul finished a project he would make a list of all the people who had actually been involved and how. Then he would update his checklist to make sure that he had included mention of the nature and impact of their involvement to be considered next time.

Working through the Stakeholder Checklist helped Paul and his project team see the big picture and get an understanding of the full scope of the project. They could see all the people and organizations involved in the project. and discuss how they might best relate to each type of stakeholder.

Managing Requirements

Paul said that he and his project team developed and used two checklists for managing requirements throughout the life of each project. The first was a short one that they used to ensure that each requirement was clearly defined. They used it to facilitate their discussions with the all stakeholders they had identified.

Requirements Review Checklist

For each listed requirement:

- Is the requirement uniquely identified?
- Is there a written statement of the requirement?
- Are all related business rules defined?
- Is every input or output described?
- Are validity checks on the inputs defined?
- Are explicitly undesired events/inputs described, along with their required responses?
- Are related user activities described?
- Are all listed performance requirements measurable?

Paul's other requirements-related checklist was for the so-called "...ilities." This checklist reminded him to review the interrelationships among the requirements and how they might affect each of those system level requirements.

...ilities Checklist:

Accessibility	Efficiency	Reusability
Adaptability	Hostility	Recyclability
Affordability	Integrity	Securability
Compatibility	Interoperability	Survivability
Compressibility	Liability	Scalability
Dependability	Mobility	Testability
Degradability	Manageability	Usability
Distributability	Producibility	Understandability
Durability	Portability	Variability

Paul said that, as each project progressed, requirements would change, and the team would use both checklists to review each change. This gave them a consistent way to assess the impact of each proposed change. The checklists helped keep them from overlooking the possible effects of each change.

15

Organizing and Delegating Tasks

Paul used his training matrix like a checklist for matching the skills of his team members with the tasks involved in the projects and delegating the work. The matrix also made it easy to match up team member skills and project tasks while he was organizing and reorganizing the work as the project progressed.

Knowing When They Were Done

Paul was particularly fond of his Project Closeout Checklist for several reasons. He quoted the project manager's version of Murphy's Law, "The first 90 percent of a project accounts for the first 90 percent of the development time. The remaining 10 percent of the project accounts for the other 90 percent."

Paul used his closeout checklist well before the end of the project to remind him of all the things he had to do for closeout. By doing that he could get most of that "other 90 percent" done before the final rush to completion.

Project Closeout Checklist:

- ☐ Conduct final review with team to ensure all deliverables have been completed and accepted.
- ☐ Make sure that the project files are complete.
- ☐ Review and document Lessons Learned with the team and prepare a report listing follow-up action that may be needed to prepare for future projects.
- ☐ Conduct and document team member performance reviews
- ☐ Update resumes and qualifications to reflect the effort.
- ☐ Prepare and deliver Completion Letter to client stating that all obligations under the contract have been met.
- ☐ Obtain response to Completion Letter from client.
- ☐ Make sure the client has paid all the invoices.

We Can All Learn from Paul

I'm glad I finally met and talked with Paul. He reminded me of how helpful checklists can be. Paul's checklists helped him remember, anticipate, address, and understand what he had to do. Using them provided him more time to focus on the substance of his projects and the work of his team. Checklists have worked well for him. You might want to develop and use checklists for yourself to get the same types of benefits.

===

===

Do you employ checklists in your daily work life, even if they're just jotted down on a sticky note? Could you live without them?

===

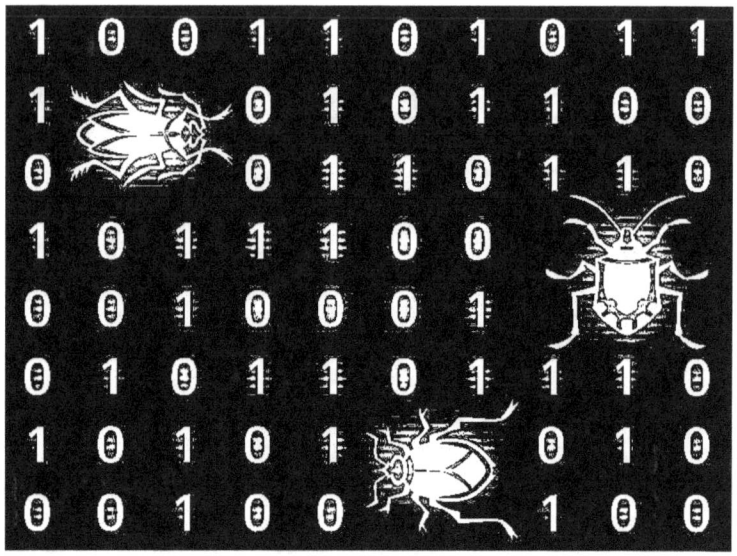

"Fleas at Work"

Specification Fleas Can Bite

Warning to all System Project Managers and Developers!

Specification fleas are those pesky things that bite you and cause you to say "Ooops!", "Ouch" or "Oh ____" when you are trying to update or change a process or a program and suddenly discover you are doing the wrong thing. These fleas hide in the formal written or informal, unwritten specifications for what you should be doing. They go after you when what you are doing conflicts with those specifications. They are related to each other in hierarchical ways, much like specifications, and they interact very much like the fleas in the poem below.

About Fleas
In the 17th Century, a British mathematician, Augustus De Morgan, wrote a poem describing fleas and the relationships among them.

> **"Great fleas have little fleas**
> **upon their backs to bite 'em,**
> **and little fleas have lesser fleas**
> **and so ad infinitum."**

The fleas in specifications are like those described by De Morgan. They come in all sizes, can exist at any level, and frequently bite each other.

About System Specifications
Formal, written specifications for systems or processes are typically prepared in the form of a hierarchy. At the top level they start with a concept. That becomes the specification for the architecture. The architecture presents an overall system or process design and provides specifications for the sub-systems and sub-processes that need to be developed to implement the design. The sub-system and sub-process designs provide specifications for components and how they are to work together. The hierarchy continues to the parts or detailed process level.

Many project teams work to unwritten or partially documented specifications. These cover all the same hierarchical levels of design and specification but are "documented" only in the minds of the participants or, occasionally, on a whiteboard in the team break room preserved with the words "Do Not Erase" written on the corner.

About Specifications Fleas

In formal specifications, fleas frequently hide under imprecise or ambiguous passages. They also lurk in incomplete corners and hide behind implicit assumptions. Others reside in sections that have not been updated since higher level designs or other circumstances have changed.

The fleas that inhabit informal specifications are, perhaps, the happiest fleas of all. They have innumerable places to live and thrive. A large colony can usually be found in the gaps of completeness. Others thrive in the areas of misunderstanding and missed communication. They can raise whole families in places where there is no consensus on the details of the specifications.

Fleas are sneaky. One must keep checking their hiding places to try to keep them away. But, no matter how hard you try, **fleas happen**!

Super Flea Killer – Fortunately, we have Arvid. He is what we call a "Greybeard." Arvid has been on many projects over the years and has seen all the different kinds of errors that people can make and the requirements and specification flaws that can make projects fail to succeed. Arvid is the one who started us calling flaws "Fleas."

Over the years, Arvid has taught our project teams how to spot fleas and deal with them. He has instilled a three-point process for flea killing. He says that when you find one you need to do three things:

 # 1 – Flea Bite Recovery: Find out where the flea bit you and treat the bite.

If there is a formal specification, check to make sure that the specification is current and correct. If it is not, correct the specification. If the specification is correct, adjust what you are doing accordingly.

If there is no formal specification, you will have to gather all involved and get full agreement on what you should be doing. (That may turn up some more fleas in what others are doing in relation to what you are doing.) After you get agreement, proceed to kill the fleas.

 # 2 – Flea Discovery: See if there are other fleas just like the one that bit you.

As in the poem, there are likely to be greater fleas and lesser fleas related to your fleas. You need to check to see if your flea was helping some other fleas to hide. You must chase them all down and kill them.

 # 3 – Flea Prevention: Go look for the places where the fleas are breeding and eliminate them.

Here you can apply systemic flea prevention treatment. Encourage formal specification documentation. Provide training in writing and reading specifications. Encourage frequent review and discussions of the design and specifications among all those involved … and take notes.

Work actively to clear up any misunderstandings. To accomplish this, some groups meet daily for design and specification discussions. Effective flea protection involves continuous aggressive flea prevention by all members of your team.

Ignore Fleas at Your Peril

"A blockhead, bit by fleas, put out the light,
And chuckling cried, "Now you can't see to bite."
Savaged by fleas he couldn't see
He quickly rued his idiocy.

Find the fleas before they find you.

===

A Tasty Treat

A "Piece of Cake"

Starting a New Project

"Hey! Piece of cake!" That was the team leader speaking after I had described the team's next project, a critical six-month, fixed price job for our top client. It was good to hear her speak so confidently, but I had some concerns.

This would be the fourth project for this team since it was formed nine months ago. They had produced excellent products on their first three projects. They worked very well, and our client gave them a pat on the back for each one. However, getting those pats on the back had not been easy for them. They had had some significant problems. They had to put in a lot of unscheduled overtime to finish those projects on time.

History

On the first project, they rushed into the work before thinking about the sequence in which tasks needed to be done. Some work not needed until later was done early and vice versa. It looked like they were doing the work backwards. They had several false starts before they figured out the right sequence. Then they had to put in extra time to get everything done.

On the second project, they had trouble figuring out what software and other materials they would need to accomplish some of the difficult tasks. They wasted a lot of time looking for those things. That put them way behind schedule. It took a lot of late nights and cold pizza (not cake) to get back on track.

On the third project, they ran into many things they never expected. Two of the key team members got sick and were out for a couple of weeks. They didn't have any slack in their schedule, so they had to work harder and longer to cover for those who were out. Some of the special software they were using didn't work properly. It took even more overtime to fix that and some other things they never anticipated.

Considering their performance on those prior projects, I decided we had better talk about the expression, "piece of cake!" because I wasn't sure that this project would be "a piece of cake." So, the next day I got them together to discuss what they would have to do.

The expression, "Piece of Cake"

I told them that this expression originated in the British Royal Air Force in the late 1930s. It was used to describe an easy mission. It evokes the easy, pleasant task of savoring and swallowing a slice of sweet dessert.

The pilots found out early on that they had to fly and survive rigors of their combat missions before they could claim that it had been a "piece of cake." On this new project, getting to the point when we can enjoy our piece of cake we will have to do what the pilots did – we'll have to go through the rigors involved in making the cake. If we do a really good job, we can all share in and eat that luscious piece of cake. So, here's a plan.

The "Piece of Cake" Project Plan

First off, we should agree on what kind of cake we are going to make. What will our final product be like? Will it be plain and simple or highly decorated? Will it contain all sorts of goodies or be very plain? We will need to agree at the outset on the vision of the cake we will all work together to make and enjoy.

Then, we'll use a cake making model as a guide. As we go through these steps, think about how these cake making tasks relate to the types of things we'll need to do on our new project.

Project Initiation
- ☐ Develop a "Making the Cake" Project Plan
- ☐ Develop a Work Breakdown Structure
- ☐ Assign tasks and due dates

Phase One – Initial Preparation
- ☐ Identify all the required ingredients
- ☐ Identify and gather all the required tools and utensils
- ☐ Find or replace any missing ingredients or utensils
- ☐ Prepare the utensils (cake pan, spatulas and mixer) for action

Phase Two - Production
- ☐ Assemble and mix the ingredients in accordance with the plan (recipe)
- ☐ Ensure all equipment is correctly set and working properly
- ☐ Grease the cake pan
- ☐ Place cake in oven
- ☐ Test readiness to deliver
- ☐ Allow time for cooling
- ☐ Perform quality review
- ☐ Avoid or mitigate risks (Ongoing Activity)

Phase Three – Delivery Preparation
- ☐ Remove "almost complete cake" from pan
- ☐ Add icing on the cake
- ☐ Package for safe delivery

Phase Four – Final Action
- ☐ Clean up utensils and kitchen
- ☐ Mark up recipe for next time

Delivery – Finally!
- ☐ Enjoy your piece of cake.

About the First Three Cakes

After we went through the cake making project task list above, we discussed, in cake-making terms, how the other three, earlier projects had gone.

Upside down Cake: On the first project, we started out with no recipe. Nobody knew what the various steps were that we had to follow so the ingredients all got mixed in the wrong order. The Work Breakdown Structure was being executed upside down. As a result, we had to do the whole project a second time to get it right.

Fallen Angel Cake: On the second project, we had confusion about the process. We didn't all agree on some of the intermediate work and that led to problems. Using the cake analogy, we forgot to include a couple of critical ingredients and that kept the product from rising to the performance level we were trying to achieve. Also, we didn't prepare properly for delivery (i.e., by greasing the pan, so to speak) so we got everything stuck at one point and some pieces crumbled as we started to get them ready for delivery.

Ouch! No Hot Mitts: On the third project, we got hurt by illness and several other unforeseen risks. We got burned by not thinking ahead about risks and allowing extra time for them. We had not ever planned a backup for our server and the power outage that killed it for two days left us with no "baking oven."

Getting to Our "Piece of Cake!"

So, now we know what we need to do. We have to make our cake before we can enjoy it. Remembering that should be easy. Spending the time and effort to do a really good job of planning and scheduling our work really pays off. It is a recipe that, ultimately, requires less elbow grease and midnight oil and makes the baking process run more smoothly. In fact, it's a:

"Piece of Cake." –

==

Yesterday, Today, Tomorrow

Yesterday

You had a disappointing project meeting. Two of your task leaders reported that they were at least a week behind schedule. One reported that his four-week task would have to be completely re-done. The only
good news was that one task had been done a week early and the other two were right on schedule. Total slippage of five staff weeks.

That was Yesterday

Today, you woke up with what is really a "new project." Your new project has the same set of deliverables and the same due date as yesterday's project. Three deliverables have had some work done on them already and you have been allocated enough time to complete them by the due date. Two other deliverables are partially complete, but both will require an extra two weeks of effort to complete properly and on schedule. One, the most disappointing one, was done wrong and that one has to be done over completely.

Your personal mantra is "Always finish each project on time on budget and with a satisfied client — No Matter What Happens." **How will you do that?**

Today

It's time for Plan B. Plan B is your plan for completing all the work still to be done. If you have some reserve staff time you can reallocate some of that and show that in Plan B. If you don't have sufficient reserves to finish in good order, plan B will have to include your plan to get what you need.

Plan B starts today and runs forward to the due date. It shows how you plan to complete all the work by then. What you heard yesterday set the starting point for your new plan. Now you have a plan to get from now to the end.

Plan B calls for another progress meeting a week from now. If all is proceeding according to the plan, Plan B will remain in effect. If there are any significant deviations from Plan B it will be time for another "new project" and Plan C.

Tomorrow

That's how this works. What happened yesterday is done and can't be undone. Forget yesterday. Solve today's problem with a plan for tomorrow.

==

==

A good project manager thinks like there is no yesterday and works like there is no tomorrow.

==

Plan B Was Yesterday

We started the project following Plan A
That only lasted a week and a day.

Then something happened that we didn't foresee.
So, we updated things and went to Plan B.

A few days passed and the team told me
Three tasks were late. So, on to Plan C.

One task recovered, miraculously
Two still were late. So we made Plan D.

A Navy order arrived requesting a lot.
So, our next revision was named Foxtrot.

Plans Foxtrot and George both went well.
But, two more tasks led to Plan Hotel.

As things kept changing we went back to letters.
Plans I, J, K, and L just sounded better.

By the end of the project we'd passed Plan Z.
Not unusual. Why? You'll see.

Each day was different from the one before
Some things were less and some things more

New team members came and some had to go.
Some tasks went fast and others ran slow.

Some risks came true and we had to adjust.
It wasn't a choice. It became a must.

Managers call it "Progressive Elaboration"
I call it "Staying tuned to the situation"

Keeping plans current is the only way.
Remember, Plan B is *"SO Yesterday"*

Bill Flury

"The purpose of a storyteller is not to tell you how to think, but to give you questions to think upon."

Brandon Sanderson

American fantasy and science fiction writer, in The Way of Kings

Section 2 - Managing

Seven stories relate to day-to-day issues that require action by a project manager to ensure success. Three of these involve dealing directly with individuals on the project team. The other four involve the whole team. Here are stories that cover both types

Individuals

Wake Up Jack – In this story, Jack gets a wake-up call and a personal priorities adjustment from his project manager.

Finish By Friday – Bob learns one of the fundamental practices required for project success **– Deliver on Time.**

Mom, Your PM Consultant – You might never have thought of retaining your Mom as a consultant on your project. But, maybe it would be a good idea.

Teams

Remote Team Conflict -Two heads are better than one except when they are butting against each other. There are ways to deal with that to ensure a successful partnership.

Ain't Doin' Right – You know what to do when your dog or cat isn't feeling well. What should you do when your project doesn't seem to be going right and no one can tell you why?

Gap Method Stimulation – Successful project managers know many ways to get things done. Here are a few tricks used by the experts.

Thunder and Lightning – We call those storms thunder storms but Lightning does the work. Who gets the credit on your projects, the person who makes the noise or the one who does the work?

===

Jack

Wake Up Jack

A Wednesday Morning Wake-Up Call

It was 10:15 a.m. and Jack, our bright, young Technical Aide, was sound asleep in his chair. This was unusual because Jack was usually a bundle of energy, bustling about and eager to help any of the senior staff. However, Jack was clearly asleep so, as gently as I could, I said, "Wake up Jack."

Jack woke up with a start and quickly apologized for drifting off. He said, "Sorry, I hope it doesn't happen again." I wondered why he was worried that it might happen again and asked him the reason. He told me why and it was a story with a lesson for all of us.

Jack's Story

Jack said that it all started a few weeks ago when he and his wife figured that they needed a bit more money. They both thought that they might be able to pick up a part time job for a couple of hours in the evenings and they both started looking. He got a lead and followed up on it with a local supermarket. The job involved spending 3 hours, 3 nights a week restocking the shelves at the market. It sounded good.

Our company had rules about "outside employment" because of concerns about proprietary data that we handled. Jack asked our Human Resources manager if it would be ok for him to take this job. Restocking shelves at the market offered no conflict so the manager gave his ok and Jack took the job.

The second job went well. Jack told me he was able to finish his regular work, get home and have a quick bite to eat, then head off to the store. He could finish by 11:00 pm and be home and in bed by 11:30. The extra money was really nice to have. Things went very smoothly for several weeks. Then, things changed a bit.

What Changed?

There was one other person doing the same part-time thing that Jack was doing, and he got sick and could not come to work. The market manager asked Jack if he could fill in for the other guy until the other guy got better. Jack figured a couple of late nights would be ok especially since it was every other night. And, the extra pay for the extra hours would be nice and it would just be for a few nights until the other guy got better.

Unfortunately, the other guy stayed sick and the manager was not able to get a replacement. Jack found that the additional hours were beginning to wear on him and told the manger that he would have to cut back to his original hours. The manager pressed him really hard to keep working the double shift.

What Happened Next?

Jack told me that the extra pay made it very attractive, so he kept on, now working until past midnight. He figured he could to tough it out. He said that so far it had worked out pretty well, but he also admitted that he had dropped off to sleep here at work one or two times before this and no one had noticed. He was sorry that he had been caught napping. He had never been in this kind of situation before. He asked for my advice.

We agreed that it didn't look like he could do both jobs well. If he cut back to his original hours at the market, he would not get the extra money, his manager would be unhappy and might even let him go. If he continued to be sleep-deprived here his work would suffer and this job might be in jeopardy. I asked him, "Which job would you rather lose?"

The choice was easy. Jack said that while it was really nice to have the extra cash from the part-time job, but he'd rather quit that than get fired from his full-time job with us. Good thinking, Jack!

The Larger Lesson

Sometimes when you are working on a project you can slip into a situation like Jack's, where you are trying to work on two things at once. For example: You are working on a long-term task that is critical to your project's success and your manager asks you to help out a team working on another task that is having a problem. Then, despite your help, some new complications arise. Their problem continues. You suddenly become the key troubleshooter working to find the solution. You dive into that and your work on your primary task starts to get neglected.

That's when you need a "Wake Up" call. That's when you need to remember Jack's story, re-think your priorities and get back to working on what's really important.

Postscript

Jack quit the market job and invested his evenings in finishing off his Associate degree at the local community college. Getting the degree led to an automatic raise, which more than made up for what he would have gotten at the market.

===

===

We often pick our priorities subconsciously. Stop and think about it for a second. Are you missing out on anything?

===

FEBRUARY

SUN	MON	TUE	WED	THU	FRI	SAT
			1	2	3	4
5	6	7	8	9	10	11
12	13	14	15	16	17	18
19	20	21	22	23	24	25
26	27	28				

www.free-printable-calendar.com

Due Date

Finish by Friday

Friday Morning

It was early Friday morning and Bob was telling me that the report he was working on was almost done and he would have it ready for me next week. He asked if that would be OK. I told him it definitely was not OK. He looked surprised, so I figured I had better explain why.

About Bob

Bob was a recently retired Air Force colonel whose most recent assignment had been at a large military software development center. He had been overseeing several long-term development projects. He had joined us a few months ago and this was his first job as a civilian defense contractor.

Bob's technical expertise was in data mining and he had successfully completed a number of internal government projects in that area. We wanted him to help us refine the requirements for a new project that we were working on for the Air Force.

About Our Project

Our project was being done on a task order that had been proposed and estimated based on careful calculations of the staff hours required for each task. The work was proposed and awarded on a fixed price basis. The task order required us to review and harmonize the data requirements as stated by four elements of our client government organization. We had done the analysis and had drafted the final report.

Bob's Task

Bob's task was to do a final review in time for us to correct any errors he might spot. We had allocated a week of his time to do that and Bob had agreed to that schedule. Up to now we were right on track to complete all of the project's tasks within the estimated number of hours. But now, Bob was telling us he would not be done until the middle of next week.

Let Me Explain

I started to explain the situation to Bob by asking him a question. I asked him how this situation would play out in the big organization he just left. Bob told me that it would be no problem. If something he was doing was due on Friday and he wasn't finished he would work as hard as he could the next week and would get the task done as soon as he could.

I asked him, "In those circumstances, would you still be in the service and getting paid for the next week?"

Bob seemed astonished by the question and said, "Certainly, why not?"

I told Bob that was different in the fixed price contractor environment. I told him that we had budgeted a certain number of hours for his task and when those hours were used there was no more money. If we were being very strict about it, and he did not finish his task by the time the money ran out there would be no more job for him and no more pay next week.

Happy Ending

That sounded pretty harsh to Bob, but he got the point. He worked through the weekend and got his report in on Monday. He thanked me for explaining how this contracting business worked – and was never late again.

==

==

Do you have team members who disregard their deadlines? Have you ever explained to them how this problem could affect them?

==

Mom – Your Project Management Consultant

A Very Busy Day at the Office

It had been a crazy morning. We had two tasks that absolutely needed to be finished today and there were still some key things that had to get done by noon. I had calls from three people that I had to put off and ask if I could talk with them later. On top of that, in 15 minutes I had to meet with a group from our main client to explain the details of the next phase. I was really frazzled.

As I started to go out of my office headed for the meeting, one of my Mom's phrases popped into my head. ***"Don't talk with your mouth full!"***

I stopped short and thought for a moment about how that was relevant. My mouth wasn't full, but my head certainly was, and I was chewing on a lot of things at the moment. If I started to talk now, whatever I was trying to say would come out all mixed up and garbled. Also, my clients could be offended when they realized that I was still thinking about other things and not giving full attention to them and their concerns.

So, following Mom's advice, I stopped chewing my current problems for a minute, swallowed hard, and quickly made a list of the five key things I had to address at the client meeting. Then, re-focused on what I was going to say, I headed off to the meeting where I gave a clear, forceful presentation that really impressed the clients.

Thanks Mom!

More from Mom

That was a great experience and a good reminder for me to remember the kinds of things my Mom used to tell us when we were kids. If you are a project manager like me, you will be amazed to see how well they relate to the things we do (or don't do) today as grown-ups. Here are a few:

1. **Getting Things Done**: If you don't do it now, when will you do it?
2. **Organizing:** If you'd put things where they belong, you wouldn't have that problem.
3. **Risk Avoidance:** Don't put that in your mouth. You don't know where it's been.
4. **Risk Mitigation:** Always wear clean underwear in case you get in an accident.
5. **Ethics:** I don't care what EVERYONE is doing. I care what YOU are doing.
6. **Honesty:** I can always tell when you're lying.
7. **Working with Others:** I don't care who started it. YOU stop it.
8. **Communications:** Don't walk away while I'm talking to you.
9. **Process Efficiency:** Turn off that light. Do you think we own the electric company?
10. **Setting Priorities:** You can go out and play after you've done your homework.

There are More

There really are many, many more of these. All of your Mom's experience in life being passed onto you in her inimitable form – and your response to most of them was, "Awwwwwww! Mom. Do I have to?" Then, you proceeded to forget them until the next time Mom got after you.

If you are fortunate, some of those, like my "Don't talk with your mouth full." will stay with you and help you succeed in your daily activities. If you want to do a quick check on which of Mom's maxims you still remember, keep track of what you are saying to your kids. —- and this time…

"If you know what's good for you, you better pay attention!"

===

What key lessons from Mom have served you well?

===

Remote Team Conflict

Eight Teams

A few years ago, I was manager of a Law Enforcement Assistance Administration project on which we had small teams working in eight different cities. Each team was tasked to work with the local police, courts, or corrections agencies to seek out and document ideas for improving operational processes or equipment. We found office space in each of the eight specified cities and relocated the team members for the full year of the project.

Each team consisted of two senior engineers. All team members were experienced senior systems engineers with strong backgrounds in operations research and information processing. In most cases they worked well together, sharing the lead on pursuing the various ideas that came up depending on their specialties. However, in three cases, strong differences of opinion emerged regarding what the pair should be focusing on. The differences of opinion became heated and I had to intervene to keep the work going forward. The root of the problem was that both team members at the problem sites had very strong different technical convictions about what they should be doing. They both considered themselves as equals and were unable to resolve their differences on their own.

Resolving the Problem

In each of these cases I had to work with the two to reach a decision based on the full scope of the project, not just their local situation (i.e., what approach would be best for all police departments, not just their police in their assigned city). Escalating the discussion to this level

41

seemed to make it easier to find a solution that would be equally satisfying (or dis-satisfying) to both. When that worked, things were fine. It did not always work. In cases where one of the original choices prevailed, I had to reassure the team member whose idea was not chosen that my decision was a business decision, not a bad mark on his technical expertise.

What We Learned

After the project was over, during our "lessons learned sessions, we discussed this situation. Some thought the escalation process that we used worked well. One person suggested that we should have designated one of the team members as the site leader at the beginning of the project, before we sent them out. Another suggested we should have had a steering group to discuss and resolve such questions. A third suggestion was to have three-person sites with one person clearly designated as the site leader. The final suggestion from this session was that, for projects like this, we should pre-brief all potential site members on this problem before they go and ask them how they will plan to resolve such situations.

==

==

What would you do?

==

Ain't Doin' Right

Looking at Your Pet

Have you ever had a pet dog or cat or bird that wasn't acting like its usual self? You probably asked it what was the problem and you never got back a Woof, Meow or Tweet about what their problem was. So, you took your ailing pet to the veterinarian. After listening to you describe how your pet was acting the vet probably said, "Your pet has ADR."

Wow! Sounds bad! But wait, what is ADR? The vet explains to you that ADR is the most common complaint that owners bring in about their pets. It is a summary of what a pet owner has observed but has not been able to interpret about what is wrong with the pet. Spelled out, the acronym means "Ain't Doin' Right." It's not at all precise but it is enough to get started on finding out the real problem.

Take Your Project to a Vet

There can be days when your project team looks and acts just like an ailing pet. You see a lack of energy, unwillingness of some team members to talk about what they are doing, and a tendency to go off into corners and avoid others. You sense that something is wrong but it's not obvious. Those are the signs that your team has ADR. It's a clear indication that it's time for you to find someone who can work with you like an animal vet, do some serious diagnosis work, find out what is causing your project's ADR, and help you figure out how to treat it. You need a Project Vet.

Dealing with ADR

My uncle lived on a farm and he rarely went to a doctor when he was feeling bad. He preferred to visit the vet because he figured that vets were better at diagnosing problems. When he went to a regular doctor the doctor would just ask him what *he* thought was the problem, give him a quick check to see if that seemed right. Then, he would give him something for that and that was that.

It's different for pets and vets. The pets can't tell the vet what's bothering them, and the owner can only voice an opinion. The vet has to dig into the situation, figure out what is wrong and then, determine what has to be done to fix it. That's the same for you and your project. Neither you nor your project team can say what's wrong, so the vet has to figure it out for you.

A vet looking at a pet with ADR will proceed by examining the patient directly for outwardly observable possible causes (e.g., a hidden sore or a strained tendon). If nothing shows up from that, the vet will then check more deeply into the possible causes of the problem. Could it be a food or feeding problem – is the pet getting enough of the right food? Might it be an environment problem – is the pet too cold or hot, bothered by noise or isolation? Perhaps it could be a relationship problem – interaction with other pets or with the owner. A good vet will pursue all of these avenues to find out why your pet Ain't Doin' Right. That's what you want your Project Vet to do for you and your project.

A Good Project Vet

When you are looking for a Project Vet you want to try to find one who has trained like an animal vet. Animal vets gain experience by working with many different species (e.g., gerbils, cats, dogs, chickens, horses, turtles). A good Project Vet will have gotten that experience by working with many different kinds of projects. Some of those projects may have been small and short-lived, like gerbils. Others may have had longer lives and been sheltered like turtles. Some may have had the discipline of a well-trained show horse or service dog. And then, there are also projects that have the unpredictable or inscrutable temperaments of cats or chickens. A good Project Vet will have seen them all.

A good Project Vet will not only have worked with different kinds of projects but will also have worked inside them. Animal vets train by doing dissections and post-mortems. A good Project Vet will have been on the inside and will have seen how the components are connected and how they flex under different stimuli.

From the inside, the Project Vet will also have observed the functioning of the different senses. An experienced Project Vet will know how teams and team members react to what they see and hear officially and via the rumor mill and how they feel about their work and their work hours and physical working environment. Animal reactions to thunder, lightning, heat and cold have equivalents in the project environment. A flash of rumors followed by rumbles of concern can be scary. The heat from the pressure of too tight deadlines can fray nerves. The cold chill of isolation from any management attention may cause a team to shiver and shake. The similarities of animal and team responses to these factors is remarkable.

Care and Feeding

Animals react in different ways to different foods. They may spurn food they don't like or scarf down their favorite. Project teams react in different ways to the kinds of work they are fed and how it is presented. An exceptional Project Vet also understands how project teams react to the "smell and taste" of the work they are doing and can figure out the different likes and dislikes of different types of project teams and how the "feedings" may need to be adjusted.

A good Project Vet also knows from personal experience the way project team members react to the way they are treated by their "owner" (i.e., management). They react poorly to being confined or being held on to short a leash, being given harsh or conflicting commands, and being left alone and isolated for a long time. On the other hand, they respond well to attention, praise for good behavior and consistent, caring treatment.

Projects have life cycles, just like animals. They start out needing lots of parenting. They may stumble and fall, get some scrapes and just need some TLC or a Band-Aid© to get over it. Then, they begin to function on their own. When they hit their teens, they may get a bit frisky and need a little extra discipline to keep from getting into trouble.

Mature animals and mature projects usually get past their teen years and become fully productive. Then, as they reach the final stages of their life they can become a bit creaky and cranky. They may need some rejuvenating treatments to continue operating or, they may need assistance to reach a graceful end.

A good Project Vet will have been through many of those cycles with many different kinds of projects, will be able to look at your project and tell you how old it is in "Project Years," and will know how it should be functioning at that stage of life and what treatments will be most effective at each stage.

When Your Project Has ADR

When your project is not going well your first reaction may be to try to figure it out on your own. You may have some ideas about the problem and start looking for a specialist to help you cure it. That's not a good approach. That's like working with a regular doctor. Whatever specialist you choose will listen to you describe the problem, help you confirm that, and give you a prescription to cure it. That's not what you need.

You need a special kind of help. – not a specialist to agree with you on what you think is wrong — you may be part of the problem. You need to go find a good Project Vet who will do a complete check-up of both you and your project.

When you go looking for a Project Vet, look for one with these good characteristics:

- Has worked with many different species of projects
- Is great at observation and diagnosis – when the patient(s) can't express what's wrong
- Knows how projects work on the inside
- Understands how project teams react to different outside stimuli
- Knows how projects function at different stages of life
- Understands you, your project, and your relationship with your project

When you get a good Project Vet you are "Doin' Right" about your project that "Ain't Doin' Right."

==

Have any of your projects needed the services of a "Project Vet"?

Gap Method Action Stimulation

A Call to Action

A stranger walks up to you and says, "Excuse me, your zipper is open."
Instinctively, you look for the exposed gap and rush to close it. Your reaction is intuitive and urgent.

Most people have a strong, inbred urge to try to close what they perceive as gaps. They feel compelled to try to fill the gap. This is the basis for what we call the "Gap Method for Stimulating Action." You can take advantage of this reaction. If you have a job to be done, find a way to display it in such a way that people will perceive it as a gap that needs to be filled.

Just getting someone to see it as a gap may be enough to draw action. When applying this method in a business situation you can include an incentive to fill the gap by identifying someone to be responsible for filling it and making the gap and the assignment public. That will add peer pressure to the incentive for filling the gap.

Defining the Gap

To help people see and act on these gaps you have to arrange things so that the gap stands out. Once they see the gaps their interest in filling them will be stimulated and action should follow.

If you doubt the strength of this impulse, you can try this example. At some place where a number of others will be passing by, write on a whiteboard or put up a sticky note showing the following:

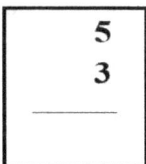

Leave it there for a while with a pencil, marker or crayon nearby. Check it later to see what has happened since you put it there.

The usual result is that someone will have filled in a plus, minus, or multiplication sign and will have completed the operation. (You may have had that urge when you were posting it.) If you were to ask people about the note, few would say that it was just a 5 and a 3 and a line. Most would have seen it as an arithmetic problem and those who did would have felt an urge to complete the problem and may have done so.

What did <u>you</u> think when you saw the 5 and 3?

The Lure of the Gap

It is instructive and fun to recall some of the ways you people can be lured into doing something by the hidden urge to fill a gap. Who does the luring? The people who want you to do something. How do they do it? They set you up by creating a situation that allows (or compels you) to see the gap and conveys a sense of urgency in getting it filled. Here are some examples.

Collecting Quarters

A few years ago the government passed The Official United States Mint 50 State Quarters, the Collector's Map®. This was custom-designed and produced for the Mint with the collector in mind. The blurb that came with it said:

> *This colorful and highly informative collector's album has many features that make it a fun and educational tool for a child, adult or the whole family! A topographical state map of the United States with push-fit holders in which to collect all 50 State Quarters from circulation. What fun for a child (or you!) to hunt for and collect each new quarter out of pocket change!*

Wow! Fifty gaps to fill. Who could resist the opportunity to fill those push-fit holes? Everyone quickly became a collector and eagerly awaited the scheduled release of the new quarter for each state.

Then, in tiny print at the bottom of the chart is this little note expanding the gap:

> ***Option to customize maps for collection of either Denver or Philadelphia mintmarks. In reality, there will be 100 quarters, not just 50! Map unfolds to over 3 feet in length!***
>
> ***How many more gaps can they create to spur sales?***

United Way

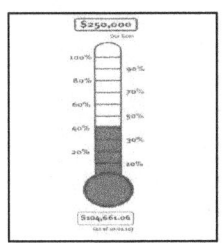

At one time or another everyone gets tapped to do some fundraising. The thermometer chart is the standard display used to help people see the gap that needs to be filled in order to meet the goal. There is a strong, visceral urge to get to the top. A Pie Chart also works, but is less effective. The way to fill the gap is less apparent.

Business Gaps

A manager trying to encourage groups to improve their performance will often present a chart like this and will ask the members of the group how they will improve their performance to bridge the gap. To make the gap more compelling, the manager can sub-divide the gap by tasks and show a detailed chart to let each team in the group see its own performance gap.

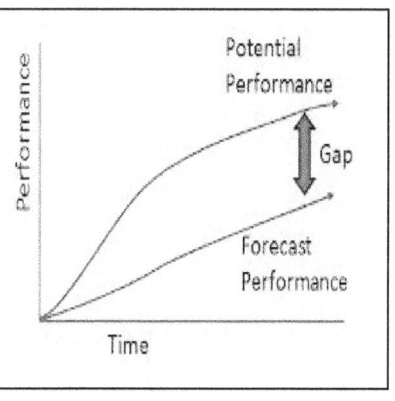

Task Completion Gaps

A Gantt chart showing task assignments, milestones, due dates, and task completions is a standard tool for showing gaps between actual and planned performance. Performance gaps can be specially highlighted by maintaining a "Today" line. Tasks planned to be done by "Today" that are to the left of "The Today Line" and are not shown to be done are late. Those are performance gaps that need to be urgently addressed.

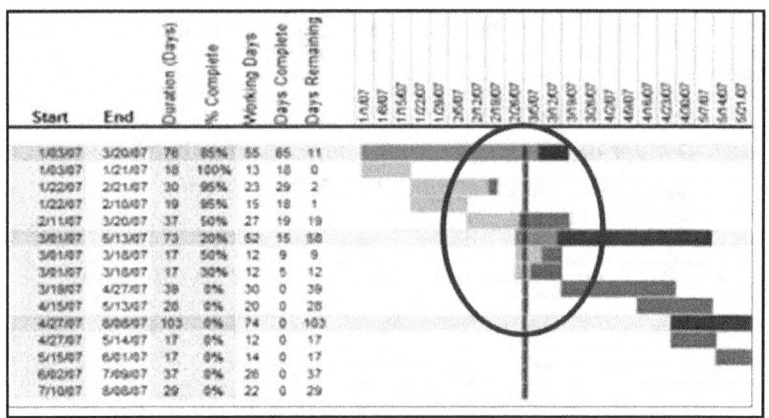

Start	End	Duration (Days)	% Complete	Working Days	Days Complete	Days Remaining
1/03/07	3/20/07	78	85%	55	65	11
1/03/07	1/21/07	18	100%	13	18	0
1/22/07	2/21/07	30	95%	23	29	2
1/22/07	2/10/07	19	95%	15	18	1
2/11/07	3/20/07	37	50%	27	19	19
3/01/07	5/13/07	73	20%	52	15	58
3/01/07	3/18/07	17	50%	12	9	9
3/01/07	3/18/07	17	30%	12	5	12
3/19/07	4/27/07	39	0%	30	0	39
4/15/07	5/13/07	28	0%	20	0	28
4/27/07	8/08/07	103	0%	74	0	103
4/27/07	5/14/07	17	0%	12	0	17
5/15/07	6/01/07	17	0%	14	0	17
6/02/07	7/09/07	37	0%	26	0	37
7/10/07	8/08/07	29	0%	22	0	29

Brainstorming Gaps

A good facilitator working with groups to help them define their business goals will not start with a blank whiteboard. That's too vague to be perceived as a gap. The expert's approach is to get the group to agree on how many goals to set and then put up a number list of blank lines. Now the gaps are more demanding. And, when all but the last two numbered lines are filled in, the final gap is really demanding.

The Gap method can be a powerful tool. When people can see the gap they will get busy and do what is needed to fill it. The key is being able to present the gap in a way that makes it easy for the viewer to see the opportunity to act.

Don't forget one of the greatest examples, in front of a church a sign that is intended to encourage attendance –

C H _ _ C H

What's missing?

==

50

Thunder and Lightning

Unfair! Unfair!

We have all experienced big *storms with lots of lightning* flashing everywhere, lighting up the sky, sometimes doing great damage, and sometimes, just crashing about from one cloud to another. What do we call these outbursts of **lightning**? We call them **thunder**storms.

This is **"Soooooooo Unfair!."** Thunder gets the top billing but it's the lightning that does all the work. We hear the thunder, but we don't immediately see what the lightning has been doing. As a result, we focus on the thunder and ignore the lightning. There's something really wrong with that. We should be focusing on what the lightning has been doing and paying attention to that.

You can experience some types of lightning and thunder on your projects. When that occurs, you need to pay attention to the lightning and not let the thunder divert your attention from what the lightning is doing.

Types of Lightning

There are many different types of lightning in nature. The principal types are:

- **Positive Lightning:** Appears to come out of nowhere and strikes downward imparting great energy wherever it lands.

- **Negative Lightning:** Goes the other way, it travels upward carrying moving energy away from the ground.

- **Cloud-to-Cloud Lightning:** Flashes from one cloud to another, expending energy in a seemingly random manner.

There can be equivalent types of lightning on your projects.

Positive Lightning – You see this when someone on your team lights up the discussion with a solution to a long-standing problem or a totally new insight into the work you are doing. In a slightly different form it may shatter a long-standing barrier to progress. It appears in a flash of brilliance and increases your prospects for success. You need to be sure that this type of lightning is accompanied by your thunderous applause. When your team hears that it will likely encourage more positive bolts from the blue.

In some cases, you may hear some loud thunder that is unfairly claiming credit for some of the positive lighting coming from others. In this situation, you need to take action to ensure proper assignment of credit.

Negative Lightning – In some cases, you may hear thunder from negative bolts. This thunder has a distinctive sound, more like a grumble than a rumble. It leads to dark clouds of pessimism and concern. It takes energy away from your project. It may wreck long-term working relationships or structures. It can cause power fluctuations, disrupt team relationships, damage morale and darken chances for team success. When you hear this type of thunder you need to track down the source and try to change the negative energy to positive.

Cloud-to-Cloud Lightning – Perhaps most troubling to you will be a continuous rumble of cloud-to-cloud mumbling that indicates a lot of energy being expended with little, if any effect. When you hear this, you will have to put on your lightning proof suit, charge out into the storm and refocus the energy from neutral to positive.

Give the Lightning Proper Credit
Look carefully at the lightning, listen carefully to the thunder and be fair. Make sure that you deal appropriately with your project's weather. Remember, the thunder is just what you hear about what's going on. You need to pay close attention to the lightning. That's what is doing the significant work.

===

How do you ensure that you are paying close enough attention to the lightning?

===

Section 3 - Controlling

Your success in business depends heavily on your ability to organize and control your work so that you can complete it all within the time available. In this section you will find nine stories about how successful people found ways to see, organize, and control their work on their projects.

See Time in a Useful Way

You will first meet Anne who initially has a problem organizing her work/time relationship but then finds a solution to her problem.

How Do You Translate Vague Specific Language?

John tells you he will be done "Shortly." When will that be? See how we deal with that on successful projects.

The Battery Free Personal Data Assistant (PDA)

Bob is a very busy guy. His success depends on his continuing to stay organized in a fast-paced and ever-changing work environment. Bob has an organizing tool that is different and is not likely to be replaced very soon by any smartphone applications or electronic Personal Data Assistant (PDA) very soon. There are three parts to Bob's story, each one with a surprise for you so be sure to keep going to the end.

A Three-foot Piece of String

It was just a piece of string, but it provided timely warning that our very big project was already in trouble and not likely to succeed.

ABCs of Scope Creep

Artur builds fences around his project's requirements. Beryl fills up the customer's gas tank with requirements. Chandra is a fan of versionizing. All three are very successful. Which one do you think could best help you manage scope creep successfully?

Ghost Meeting

They met at 3:30 p.m. in the conference space to address three issues of concern to all of them. The discussion was very focused. They agreed on how each of the issues should be addressed and the actions that would be required to resolve them. One week later, the same group met and held what amounted to the same meeting they had had the week before. It seemed as if the prior meeting was a ghost – it had never occurred. How did that happen?

Yesterday, Today Tomorrow

A project manager awakens each day with a new situation. Some scheduled tasks have been done. Some have not. However, by the end of the project the promised product must be delivered. How do successful project managers deal with that?

Plan B Was Yesterday – Re-planning

Successful project management requires continuous re-planning. This is a poem that illustrates how that worked for a fictional project.

A Well-Organized Group - Finally

The organization was a 60-person contractor organization that was responding to government requests for changes to a large database. Over 50 such requests had to be handled each month. There was a company manual for handling change requests that included a detailed, step by step description of how it should be done. All of the staff had been trained in the official life cycle. However, they had a problem. Despite the manuals and the training, everyone did his work a bit differently. Their process was chaotic, and they had a lot of their work rejected.

This story tells about the unusual way they resolved their problem and achieved a successful solution.

==

Now, on to the stories ....>

See Time in a Useful Way

You should really meet Anne.

Anne is someone who used to think that a 24-hour day was too short. She never seemed to be able to get done all the things she had to do or should have been doing within the time available. She worked hard and long, ate at her desk while she worked and slept less than Mom always told her she should. Even with all that, she still couldn't get everything done.

Anne did get a lot done but there were some important things she should have been doing to build her business that she never seemed to be able to get to. She needed to find a way to squeeze those things into her day. In her story you will see how she solved her problem by finding a way to see and seize the snippets of time she needed. You might want to do the same.

See Anne See and Seize Snippets of Time

Anne is a real estate agent who specializes in commercial sales. She learned her business by watching other agents. She was mentored by one of the older ones through the first several months. She did well but always felt rushed and always had a hard time fitting all the phone calls she had to make into her day. With the phone calls as a priority, she often had to work late to get all her other work done.

When we first talked, Anne said she desperately wanted to find a way to make better use of her time. She had been thinking about what she was doing, and it was all sort of a blur. She was always busy (e.g., meetings, paperwork, calls, conferences) and she wasn't able to see any "empty" moments. Anne felt that if she could find such moments she would be able to squeeze into them some of the things she now had to do after the end of her normal workday.

In our first discussion we talked about the importance of being able to actually see how she spent her time rather than just thinking about it. We agreed that that was the key to finding ways to make better use of her time. We both felt that when she could see the whole picture she would be able to spot some unproductive and wasted moments and would be able to put them to better use.

Setting the Time Trap

Anne agreed to take a few minutes each morning to prepare a "Today Sheet." She would list her scheduled appointments, follow-up telephone calls and other planned tasks for the day in the order in which she expected to do them. She would also estimate the time she thought each task was likely to take.

Anne also agreed to take a few minutes right after lunch and at the end of the day to record the actual amount of time each planned task took and to record what she did with the "free" time if the task took less time than planned. Anne understood that is was going to require some effort, but she resolved to do this for a couple of weeks and then we would take a look at the results together to see what was happening. We both hoped that when she could see the spare moments in her day, she could make better use of them.

Checking the Time Trap

As Anne got into it, she began to realize how often things didn't always go as planned. There were variations. Sometimes some of the things she did took less time than she thought they would. A meeting might get cancelled or getting some rental documents ready might take less time than usual. Those situations seemed to yield what she was looking for – the "extra" moments that she might capture and use.

After two weeks of tracking we reviewed her notes together. We discovered several things:

First, there were many unplanned "free" moments that occurred every day. We called those moments of time "snippets."

Second, she saw that what she was usually doing in those snippets was checking her e-mail and the latest news. Neither of those activities was very productive. She really did not need to do these any more than twice a day, and here she was, doing them every time she had a free moment. When she added up the time she was spending on those, the total came to almost an hour a day of time that might be put to better use if she could find a way.

We began to look for useful things that she had to do that were small enough to fit into those five to ten-minute snippets of time that she had discovered. She found a number of things that could be done at any time during the day and usually only took a couple of minutes each. She made a list:

- Next Day Prep – Reviewing contact sheets for the next day's appointments
- Inventory Walk – Reviewing the list of available properties
- Lead Follow-Up – Calling new leads
- "Bird Dogging" – Prospecting for leads by calling friends and associates
- Making follow-up calls to clients to whom she had sold something

As we reviewed the list, we agreed that the first three things were so important that she should schedule time to do them. The last two items were the important things for which she never seemed to have enough time. Maybe we could find out how to fit those into her spare moments.

Preparing to Use Snippets of Time

The problem with trying to make better use of time snippets is that you can't be sure when they will occur. They just pop up and you have to be ready to take advantage of them. You can't predict when a meeting will run short, when traffic will be less than expected, or when any of the other "snippet producers" may occur.

Anne figured out that in order to be ready to do make use of the snippet time, she would have to have a handy list of potential calls that she could make when the opportunities arose. So, she added a few minutes to her schedule each morning to update her call lists for "Bird Dogging" and Follow-Ups with past clients. She kept those with her throughout the day and used them whenever she had a spare moment.

Over the next few weeks, Anne found that changing what she was doing was not as easy as she thought. The siren call of e-mails and news feeds was very strong, and she had to remind herself to go to her call lists first – before getting distracted. However, as she gradually worked into the routine, she began to see that she was making more calls and getting good results from that.

Anne was convinced. She continued to use her Today Sheet as a window into her activities. It helped her see what she was doing and understand where and how she could make what she was doing work better.

Seeing Time

At the outset, Anne knew there must be moments that she could capture and use more productively, but she could not see them. Anne had to find a way to make time visible. She did that by starting and maintaining a physical record of her time: how she planned to spend it and how she actually spent it.

Anne's written "Today Sheet" was a tabular record. Her daily records provided snapshots of her activities and enabled her to see and analyze the details of her work patterns and habits. Once she could see "snippets of time," Anne was able to change her habits and get prepared to seize and use those moments when they occurred. You could do that!

===

===

"If you want to make good use of your time, you've got to know what's most important and then give it all you've got."

Lee Iacocca

===

Vague Specific Language

The Situation

A deadline is approaching. You are checking your project schedule and see that John's task is due to be finished a week from today. You catch up with John and the following conversation ensues:

You: "John, your task is due next Wednesday. When will you be done?'
John: "Shortly"

You, "Are you having any problems?"
John: "A lot of small ones, but no show stoppers?"

You: "So, when do you think you'll finish?"
John: "In a few days or so, probably by Tuesday."

You: "Can I count on you to finish on time?"
John: "Absolutely! I'm 100% certain."

Will John Finish On Time? What Do You Think?

John is speaking in a language that is best called *"Vague-Specific."* This is a form of language in common use by many. Here are some examples of how it works.

The Long-Time Married Couple: When they are headed out for a night at the theater, one spouse will say, "Are you ready to go?" The other will respond, "I'll be down **shortly."** Over the years they have come to a mutually understood Vague-Specific meaning of **shortly** and the spouse who asked the question plans to be ready to go out the door in approximately 7 ½ minutes.

The project team that has worked together for a long time: Through time, the team has defined many of its own important terms. One group has developed a set of Vague-Specific terms to express the amount of time it is likely to take to resolve some of the types of problems that are common in their work. They have agreed on the following: **Small** (2-3 hours to resolve); **Medium** (4-8 hours to resolve), and **Large** ("We'd better discuss it."). This works for them.

Understanding Common Vague Specific Terms

Researchers have done several serious studies of how and why people use the Vague-Specific language. They use it when they are unable or unwilling to be accurate and specific, or they think it is unnecessary or inappropriate to do so.

Expressing Time: In web discussions of Vague-Specific definitions and values you will find some wonderful ways of expressing time.

- **Presently**: When *immediately* is over and before **Soon**. (See Also: *in the near future; before long; in a little while*). There are also some old terms for this: *in the twinkling of an eye; before you know it and; in a jiffy.*

- **Soon**: May be interpreted differently in different regions. It means whatever number of hours, days, or weeks is commonly acceptable in the local environment. In a fast-paced city environment **Soon** might be *"in a New York Minute"* (itself a Vague-Specific term) and in a relaxed environment it can mean *"When I'm not busy with all the other things I'm doing"* – and that could be days or weeks away.

- **Shortly**: Synonym for **Soon**.

- **Later**: Pretty well covered by **Soon** and **Shortly** but can be after that.

Expressing Quantities:

- **One:** Almost always means just one and is pretty specific. However, it is often paired with other terms that make it vaguely specific. Example: "I'll give you just one more chance." Or, "I'll be there in one hour."

- **Few**: This is more than a couple (commonly 2-4, as in a couple of days) and can be up to five.

- **A Lot:** When someone says they have a **lot** of problems they typically mean somewhere between 6 and 10 and, if they say "**a whole lot**" they may be telling you they have as many as 17.

Expressing Problems Size:

- **No Big Deal –** Negligible, unless it is clear that the speaker hasn't really looked into it, in which case, see **Large**.

- **Small:** This type of problem will take 2-3 hours to resolve.

- **Medium:** This type of problem usually requires 4-8 hours to resolve.

- **Large:** All problems are **Large** unless the speaker/writer is willing to admit that they are really either **Small** or **Medium**.

- **Show-Stopper:** This is used for problems requiring more resolution time than we have left to address and resolve. (Often characterized in texting as **OMG!**)

Expressing Probabilities:

Barry Boehm, in his 1989 book, *"Software Risk Management"* presented the results of his formal study of what people really mean when they express the probability of occurrence of software development project risks. Here is what he found:

- Almost Certain, Highly Likely: 85-100%
- Probably, Likely: 55-85%
- Better Than Even: 50-55%
- Almost No or Little Chance: 5-25%
- Slight, Highly Unlikely: 1-15%
- No Way: 0.1-1%

Will John Finish His Task On Time?

Let's now review your discussion with John. Let's fill in values for the Vague-Specific terms that John used in his answers:

You: "John, your task is due next Wednesday. When will you be done?'

John: "Shortly"

In John's work group, **Shortly** has come to mean "in a few (3-5) days." There are five workdays between now and next Wednesday and there's also a weekend so meeting the deadline seems pretty safe.

You, "Are you having any problems?"
John: "A lot of small ones, but no Show Stoppers?"

John has a **lot (6-10)** of **small (2-3 hours to resolve)** problems and no medium or Show Stoppers for a maximum of 30 hours of known problem resolution time. As above, there are 40 regular work hours available before the deadline so it still looks good as long as John doesn't have a "whole lot" of problems. That could require up to 51 hours of problem resolution time.

You: "So, when do you think you'll finish?"
John: "Probably in a couple of days or so."

John says it is **probable (55-85%)** that he will finish in a couple of days (usually 2-5 but a maximum of 7) of days or so and the **"or so"** might add a day or two to his estimate. In the past, John's "couple of days" has usually meant four. We can be optimistic and assume that there is an 85% chance that he will finish within the deadline in four days or, we can be pessimistic and assume that there is only a 55% chance of being done in four days. Meeting the deadline is beginning to look a little shaky, so we better check one more time.

You: "Can I count on you to finish on time?"

John: "Absolutely! I'm 100% certain."

You need to know that, in all the time that John has been on the team he has never missed a deadline so let's give him credit for being 100% certain and we will expect him to finish on time. **However, we'll check again on Monday.**

Learning to Live with The Vague-Specific Language

If vagueness is a problem and specifics are important to you or your work, here are a **couple** of things you should do: (*Remember that a couple can be 2-4, sometimes as many as 5.*)

- **Be aware of the extent of its use:** The Vague-Specific is used everywhere. Watch for it to appear in all forms of written and spoken communication. Learn to live with it.

- **Learn the local dialect:** Tune in to the way Vague-Specific is being used where you live and work. Make sure that everyone agrees to a common vocabulary and the same definitions for all of the terms you and they use. Work hard to:

  - Hear and understand what others are really saying. Build your own mental dictionary and calibrate the terms they are using

  - Adjust your own language to the local definitions so that you are correctly understood by others

- **Minimize the underlying reasons for its use:** Find ways to demonstrate the ways that being more specific will aid communication and reduce misunderstandings and confusion. Work with the Vague-Specific speakers and writers to encourage and enable them to be more specific.

===

Will these things help? — Probably.

What vague-specific terms have you heard over the years?

===

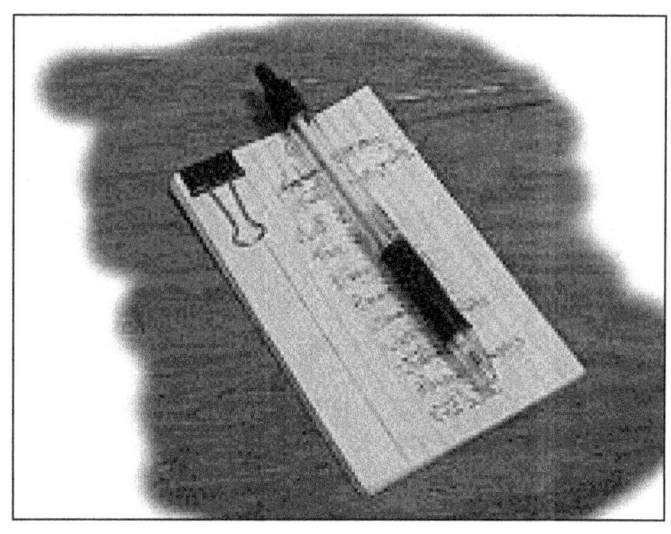

World's Most Reliable PDA

World's Most Reliable PDA *

See reader warning at end.

My Smartphone Gasped and Died

"Help! Send power!" I was stuck with a lot of things on my schedule and a lot of contacts to call and my phone wouldn't let me in to see what I had to do next. I went to see Mary in the office next door and she loaned me a charging cord. She empathized with my predicament and then, with a laugh, she said, "You need to talk with Bob. Bob has a battery-free PDA and he never gets into a fix like this."

The Battery Free Personal Data Assistant (BFPDA)

She said that Bob uses what he calls his "Battery Free PDA" to plan for and keep track of the things he has to do. He started using his BFPDA in his early working years and has been using and refining it since then. He claims that no single app or combination of apps on current PDAs or smartphones can do it better for him.

She told me that Bob is not impressed with a lot of the new technology that looks like it is supposed to do wonderful things but really is hard to use and delivers very little for all the effort it requires. He is very, very practical. He favors things that are easy to use, are reliable, and help him do useful things efficiently – and his cell phone apps don't meet any of those criteria.

Talking with Bob

I tracked down Bob and we talked. Bob told me that he uses his BFPDA to record all the tasks he wants to accomplish each day, meetings he needs to attend, keep track of where he has to go, calls he has to make, any ideas that happen to pop into his head, and special notes to himself.

Everything he needs to know about his day is visible, in one place, all the time. He sees everything that he has to be concerned with each day in a way that makes it easy for him to understand what he has to be doing as the day progresses. Bob admitted that he does use some phone apps for things that they do best (e.g., phone calls, e-mail, lookup, map and travel info). He has integrated the use of those apps with his BFPDA in a seamless way.

65

BFPDA vs. Conventional PDA

Bob really enjoyed telling me about the many ways that the BFPDA is better for him than the current crop of PDAs and their related apps on smartphones. It is completely battery-free. It uses no electricity and never needs to be charged. Bob doesn't have to worry about battery levels, carry a charger, or worry about where he can find an outlet for charging. It can be operated anywhere, even in places with no electricity within miles. It's great for people traveling in remote areas. The BFPDA is always ready. Bob went on to describe the key features in several categories.

Data Entry

All data entry is manual. The BFPDA surface is rugged. Data entry can be made with a pen, pencil, marker, or even a crayon if nothing else is available. The data entry method is particularly good for Bob. Bob did not grow up using a keyboard, especially one as small as the one that pops up on his smartphone. Pencils work just fine for him and he always has one handy. There is no limit on the amount of data that can be entered and no carrier data plan charges for any amount of storage. Additional storage is readily available if needed and is very inexpensive.

Technical Reasons – Lots of Them

- All of the data on the BFPDA are always available at a moment's notice. No need to tap an app icon or press a button. There is no wait time for an app to fire up.

- Backup is automatic. The original is preserved and must be manually erased to get rid of it.

- You can lose it or drop it in water, but your chances of recovery are a lot better than if you did the same with a conventional PDA

- Nobody is likely to steal the BFPDA.

- If the BFPDA does get stolen the thief doesn't get your whole life history and personal data.

- Nobody can trace your whereabouts or mine data from the BFPDA electronically.

- It can be used in areas where highly classified work is being done and electronic devices are prohibited.

- You never have to shut off the BFPDA during a meeting. In fact, you can use it during meetings and even refer to it during the performance of a show or movie without disturbing others.

You may be surprised to learn about some of the other reasons Bob likes the BFPDA.

Personal Reasons

- Nothing Extraneous – The "picture" of the day is never cluttered up by all your e-mails and internet "stuff."

- No Temptation to Waste Time – When you are using the BFPDA there is no temptation to check your e-mail or surf for news or any of the other time wasters that PDAs lure you into. It protects you from being drawn into those time-wasting activities.

Surprise!

While reading all about this wonderful invention you have likely been wondering how it could possibly work. At last, we can reveal the secret.

Bob's BFPDA is a set of 3 x 5 note cards that he keeps in his shirt pocket along with his smartphone in the place where Bob's vinyl pocket protector used to reside in his early working days.

Bob keeps and maintains his list of pending tasks on the cards. At the top of the deck is the "Today" card. It lists all of the tasks that he wants to accomplish today. Bob notes on the card all the tasks he wants to accomplish for the day. These notes are words or phrases that remind him of each task that he will try to finish today. On the right-hand side of the card Bob lists the places he has planned to go to during the day (e.g., doctor, bank, Staples). The Today Card provides a complete picture of where Bob has to go and what he expects to accomplish during the day.

As the day progresses and Bob goes places and does things he strikes out the items on the card to show that they have been done and adds new items as they come up. Bob follows a disciplined Today Card maintenance process. At the end of the day he checks to see what he has completed (think "sense of satisfaction or disappointment") and creates a Today Card for the next day.

How Much High Tech Do You Really Need?

A while back a California blogger posted an article in which he commented, "The number of gadgets folks lug around is creeping ever upward, but do you really need to carry $1,000 worth of equipment to have coffee with friends and be able to write down what albums you should check out?"

His target was a generation of digital natives that has been trained to instinctively believe that technology can solve all of a person's problems. He wanted to show them that high-tech solutions are not always the best answer.

To draw the interest of his techie readers, he thought up a techie sounding name, the Hipster PDA (hPDA), and went on to characterize it as a *marvelous new invention*. It turned out to be a stack of 3×5 cards held together with a binder clip – just like Bob's. The blog item went viral and the blogger was surprised by the reaction.

Bob Is Not Alone

In response to the blog, thousands of Bobs "came out" and admitted that they also found that the cards worked better for them than the fancy apps on their phones. Sensing potentially large market, specialty websites sprang up selling 3 x 5 card templates and techniques.

Many users are now exchanging tips on Internet mailing lists. On Flickr there are almost 200 photos of versions of the BFPDAs/hPDAs in use, made by users around the world. The folks using these homemade organizers are not Luddites; in many of the shots, laptops, fancy cell phones and digital cameras clamor for space alongside the index cards. They are people who are not hypnotized by the technical hype and have, instead, made a rational decision to use what works best for them.

Looking to the Future

Now, a marriage of the BFPDA concept and the phone apps is in the offing. In September 2013, one company announced a new product that will bring the Bobs and the digital natives closer together, both figuratively and literally. You can now buy sticky note pads tailored to fit on the back of your iPhone. Bob is likely to be the first in line to buy them and you may not be far behind.

*Warning: The contents of this article may be disturbing to Digital Natives (i.e., persons born since the invention of the internet).

==

==

What is your preference? PDA, BFPDA, or a combination?

==

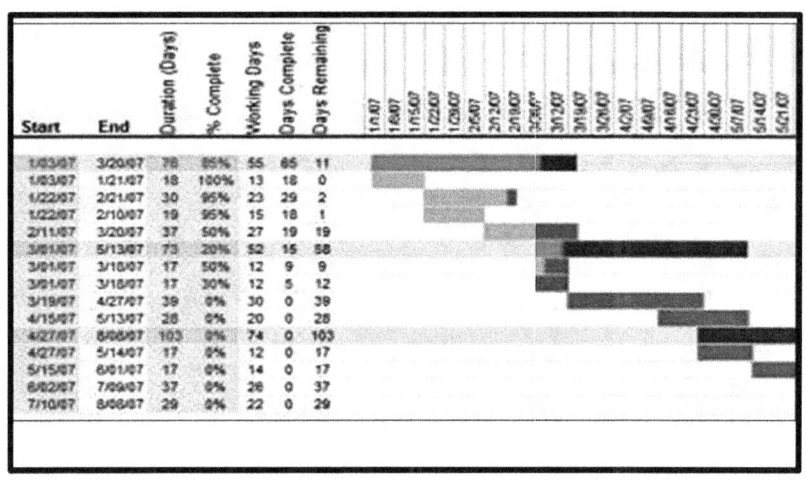

Start	End	Duration (Days)	% Complete	Working Days	Days Complete	Days Remaining
1/03/07	3/20/07	78	85%	55	65	11
1/03/07	1/21/07	18	100%	13	18	0
1/22/07	2/21/07	30	95%	23	29	2
1/22/07	2/10/07	19	95%	15	18	1
2/11/07	3/20/07	37	50%	27	19	19
3/01/07	5/13/07	73	20%	52	15	58
3/01/07	3/18/07	17	50%	12	9	9
3/01/07	3/18/07	17	30%	12	5	12
3/19/07	4/27/07	39	0%	30	0	39
4/15/07	5/13/07	28	0%	20	0	28
4/27/07	8/06/07	103	0%	74	0	103
4/27/07	5/14/07	17	0%	12	0	17
5/15/07	6/01/07	17	0%	14	0	17
6/02/07	7/09/07	37	0%	26	0	37
7/10/07	8/06/07	29	0%	22	0	29

Project Plan

70

A 3 Foot Piece of String Can Save Your Project

A Big Project

We were getting going on a major system conversion process. Our job was to replace a legacy image processing system with all new hardware and software. Our team included three contractors, one for software, one for the computing hardware and one for displays. We were in the third month of an 18-month schedule. The project had been planned by the combined team and the schedule and tasking was recorded on-line in MS Project. We had a "War Room" with a giant Gantt chart on the wall showing the detailed task schedules for each of the 187 tasks involved in the project. We had regular meetings in the War Room where we reviewed that large chart and discussed the progress on the project.

Trouble Ahead?

We were only in the third month, but I had a vague feeling that the project was beginning to slip. We had recently read a US Air Force study that showed that projects that were behind schedule at the 15% mark never recovered their slippage. The study was based on hundreds of their projects. Those that were behind at this point never got better and usually slipped even more. That made us nervous because we were now at the 15% point. If we had slippages now, we would have to struggle to keep from having a big overrun.

We had been meeting every other week to discuss schedule and each contractor Task Manager was saying that things were ok. We kept hearing, "One or two tasks might be lagging but we're ahead on the others so, were fine." After two or three meetings like this the PM decided that we had to find out what was really happening. All it took to highlight our problems was a 3-foot piece of red string. How could such a simple thing as a piece of red string become a powerful project management tool? Here's how.

On the 15th of November we went to the project Gantt chart and fixed the top of the string to the 15 November mark on the schedule line. We ran the string straight down to the bottom and taped it in place. We called the piece of string the "Today Line."

What the Today Line Did for Us

Immediately, it became clearly apparent that all unfinished tasks to the left of "Today" were late and we could see how many there were. Also, glaringly obvious, was the fact that there were not enough "work-aheads" to the right to balance the late tasks. The contractors' game of "We're fine" was over. Now, for the first time, instead of dealing with a broad look at our progress we could all see the lateness problem on a task-by-task basis and start to deal with the total picture.

We thought, and later figured out, that they were playing a game of "Chicken." Each one waited for another to own up to a slip in one of their tasks. Then, they could all claim that they were being held up by the other person who admitted a slip.

We moved the line each day and discovered that, in addition to its ability to stop the game-playing with the progress reporting, it also provided new and compelling motivation to the task leaders for those whose lagging tasks were now so obviously apparent to the left of "Today." Another bonus was the opportunity for us to recognize the task leaders who were consistently ahead of schedule.

In a children's book by Marion Holland called, "Big Ball of String" an imaginative CAN-DO 6-year-old child says, "With a BIG ball of string I could do ANYTHING, anything, anything, ANYTHING AT ALL." That child has a good start on becoming a successful project manager.

Establishing and enforcing schedule discipline in a project doesn't require a BIG ball of string. A three-foot piece called the "Today Line" is all you need to start.

===

Do you have a clever process of your own to help keep your teams on schedule?

===

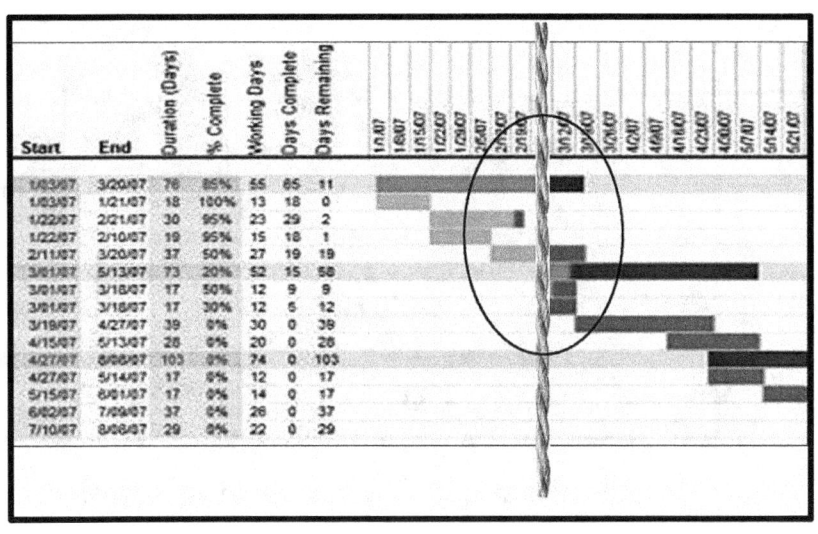

Start	End	Duration (Days)	% Complete	Working Days	Days Complete	Days Remaining	1/1/07	1/8/07	1/15/07	1/22/07	1/29/07	2/5/07	2/12/07	2/19/07	3/12/07	3/19/07	3/26/07	4/2/07	4/9/07	4/16/07	4/23/07	5/7/07	5/14/07	5/21/07
1/03/07	3/20/07	76	85%	55	65	11																		
1/03/07	1/21/07	18	100%	13	18	0																		
1/22/07	2/21/07	30	95%	23	29	2																		
1/22/07	2/10/07	19	95%	15	18	1																		
2/11/07	3/20/07	37	50%	27	19	19																		
3/01/07	5/13/07	73	20%	52	15	58																		
3/01/07	3/18/07	17	50%	12	9	9																		
3/01/07	3/18/07	17	30%	12	6	12																		
3/19/07	4/27/07	39	0%	30	0	39																		
4/15/07	5/13/07	28	0%	20	0	28																		
4/27/07	8/06/07	103	0%	74	0	103																		
4/27/07	5/14/07	17	0%	12	0	17																		
5/15/07	6/01/07	17	0%	14	0	17																		
6/02/07	7/09/07	37	0%	26	0	37																		
7/10/07	8/06/07	29	0%	22	0	29																		

Project Plan with TODAY Line

73

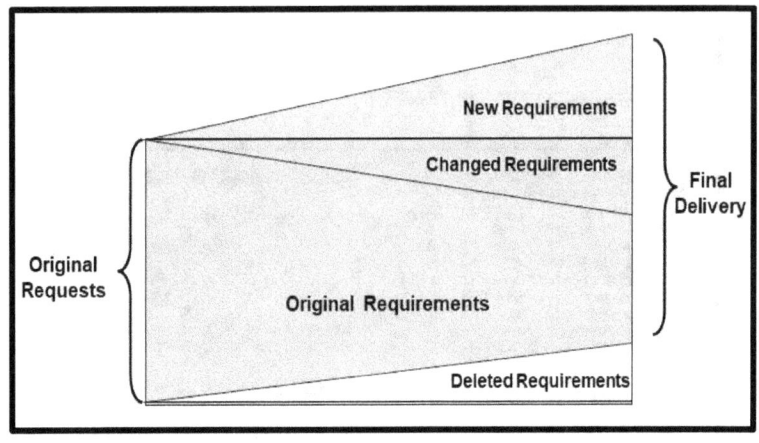

Requirements Change During a Project

The ABC's of Scope Creep Management

Sharing Ideas

Three experienced project managers were having coffee together in a break room at a Project Management Institute workshop on Scope Management. Their workshop moderator had asked them to share scope creep stories about their clients and their projects. They all had "inventive" clients who  were very prone to requesting new work or changes to task lists to which they had originally agreed. They all felt that they were doing a good job in controlling that situation but, as it turned out, each one was doing it in a different way.

Artur's Story: Artur was a stickler for tight control. He told the others that he worked very hard at the beginning of his projects to nail down the requirements. He always made sure that each task was well defined and documented. He called that process "erecting fences." As his projects progressed and his client started to ask for things outside the fences he would work up a change order stating how much work would be involved and indicating the cost implications.

Artur said that he felt that that was the safest way to handle the requests and it was the approach that was being proposed in the workshop. He told the others that it worked well from a business standpoint, but his client really did not like it. His client was always fussing about being "nickeled and dimed" and would always complain about all the paperwork involved in each change. He was always asking, "Why can't you just go ahead and do what I asked and send me a bill at the end?"

All three at the table agreed that tight control was important, and they began to discuss ways to make everybody involved feel better about it.

Beryl's Story: Beryl chimed in. She said that she and her client were working well and happily together. They had discussed the potential for scope creep and had decided on a slightly different way to handle requested changes.

When she was planning her project, Beryl set aside a substantial reserve of staff hours to cover changes and risk mitigation. She told her client about the reserve and that she had set aside half of it for him. She told him how many hours were in his part of the reserve and asked him to think about it like gas in a gas tank. They agreed to keep the gas gauge hours visible on the project web site. Each time her client requested a change she would get back to him with an estimate of how much of the reserve "gas" he would be using. Then, the client could decide if he wanted to take the trip. He also had the option of getting out his credit card and putting more gas into the tank if he wanted to extend the trip.

Beryl's client liked this approach. It did not have that nickel-dime feeling. It was a pleasant way of sharing the responsibility for controlling and paying for changes.

Chandra's Story: Chandra's projects were all software projects. She told the others that she and her client had agreed on a different approach. In their approach, all changes would be accepted without question. The only thing they ever had to discuss was timing.

Chandra explained the method they used. The day after they started work on Version # 1 of the product, they would designate someone to start recording the features that will be in Version # 2. This way, they never had to say, "We need more money to pay for it" or "We can't do it!" They would agree that the requested feature will be in the next version. If there was any quarrel with that, they would discuss how to swap some of V#1 into V#2 to keep things in balance. This approach worked for Chandra and Chandra's customer was happy with it.

Their Class Presentation

During the break the three had shared three very different approaches to managing scope creep and were ready to head back into the workshop. There, they would tell the others about their conversation and the A B C's of their approaches.

Beryl was chosen to speak for all three. She went to the whiteboard and wrote this:

Here are the A B C's of managing Scope Creep

- **A**rtur's Fences
- **B**eryl's Gas Tank
- **C**handra's Version Control

Then Beryl described each approach as they had discussed them in the break room. There was some discussion of the drawbacks and benefits of each of them. After that, the moderator asked each member of the workshop "**Which method would work best for you?**"

==

==

Which of these approaches would work best for you?

==

Last Week's Meeting

Ghost Meeting

They Met at 3:30 p.m.

Yesterday, four people met in the conference space to address three issues of concern to all of them. The agenda had been circulated beforehand, so the discussion was very focused. They agreed on how each of the issues should be addressed and the actions  that would be required to resolve them. At the end of the meeting, as everyone was heading out the door to get back to work, the leader congratulated them on their analysis and discussion.

One week Later

After a hectic seven days, the same group came together and held what amounted to the same meeting they had had the week before. Nothing had changed except the calendar. The issues they discussed were the same, the proposed resolutions were the same. It seemed as if the prior meeting was a ghost – it had never occurred.

How did that happen?

Well, for one thing, at the earlier meeting no one kept any notes of the discussion and the decisions. Everyone remembered the discussions but not very well and differently. So, they had to discuss the issues again to reach agreement, again.

The tasks they agreed on were not written down so each (very busy) person was willing to believe that someone else was the one responsible. The manager, also very busy, had no basis for following up to make sure the agreed upon tasks were being done. The tasks did not get done. So, they started to hold the same meeting again. How wasteful and annoying that would be!!

They Saw the Ghost

A few minutes into the meeting they saw the ghost of the previous meeting. They decided to figure out how keep from having any more ghost meetings. After some discussion, they developed a **Ghostbusting Checklist** and make it mandatory for all meetings.

Appoint a ghostbuster who will:

1. Keep a copy of the agenda

2. Keep notes on the essence of the discussions and decisions

3. List all action assignments and due dates

4. Promptly, after the meeting, provide a copy to the leader of the meeting for follow-up.

5. And, if you are the leader, follow up on all action assignments.

6. ==

==

Advice: If you want to break records, make records.

==

==
Special Note: This article is based on my experience in support of the White House Office. We were retained to attend the meetings of senior staff in the Roosevelt room of the West Wing. Our job was to take notes – specifically listing all tasks, agreed due dates and person responsible. Within a few hours of the end of the meeting we would provide the convener of the meeting with a notebook with listings by person, by due date and by subject.

On the day after the meeting we would visit the convener and show him/her how to use those listings to follow up when making phone calls to the various attendees. In effect, we were training them to be good project managers. Most of them were policy and idea people and had never had PM experience.

Until we started doing this they had been having lots of ghost meetings. The presidential initiatives and legislation they were working on had stalled. That finally changed, and the initiatives began to achieve some forward momentum.

==

==

"Words are how we think; stories are how we link."

Christina Baldwin

==

Section 4 - Risk

Here we have stories about project risks. Success as a project manager requires the ability and determination to anticipate, identify, assess, plan for, and deal with as they arrive.

Project managers are tasked with completing their assigned tasks, satisfying their clients, and completing on time and within budget. They are expected to do this no matter what happens. Thus, effective risk management is a critical skill they must master.

Risks of Project Management and Skiing

This story is about a project manager who always has risk on his mind. Even while he is on vacation he is thinking about risk. You'll be interested to see the parallels he finds between project management risks and skiing risks.

Your Toughest Project

At a company retreat, a session facilitator asked the attendees to describe their toughest projects. Three experienced project managers told their stories. All of the projects were very difficult. You can decide which you think would have been the most difficult for you to complete successfully.

Titanic Problems

The Titanic was unsinkable. All the potential risks had been carefully considered and mitigations had been prepared for each (e.g., watertight compartment doors, Special lookout stations). The builders had prepared for each one but not for simultaneous occurrence of many. In subsequent investigations it was determined that there were 13 simultaneous failures that doomed the ship. This story may spark your thinking about multiple failures on your projects.

==

Risky Business

Skiing and Project Management Risks

Skiing is Inherently Risky

If you are a skier, you know that there are many risks involved in every run. You face challenges at every turn and face loss of control or failure throughout every run. When you go skiing, you are reminded of all the inherent risks by the slope managers who provide you with a handy list on the back of your lift ticket.

There is a caution printed on the back of lift tickets at all Utah ski sites. It is wise to read it before going on the slopes and remember to be prepared for all of the contingencies listed.

Project Management is Also Inherently Risky

As a project manager you also know that there are many risks involved in every project. You face challenges at every turn and face loss of control or failure throughout every project. Each time you start a new project it would be helpful to have a handy reminder of the inherent risks that you must be prepared to face.

The types of risks mentioned on the ski ticket might be the same that you face when you are managing a project. See how they might apply:

A Skiers Tips for Project Managers

So how can Project Managers ensure safety and progress on the slopes? When you return from your ski vacation, keep your lift ticket handy. Put it some place where you will see it often and learn from the wisdom of the slopes. As you manage your projects, stay aware of the risks of:

- The surface weather and terrain
- Subsurface conditions
- Fixed, unmovable objects
- Others on the same slopes
- Your own abilities related to the situation

If you cannot accept the inherent risks of project management, don't get on the slopes.

===

Inherent Risks of <u>Skiing</u> -- Definitions

"Inherent risks of Skiing" means those dangers or conditions which are an integral part of the sports of skiing, snowboarding, and ski jumping, including, but not limited to:

- Changing **weather** conditions
- Variations or **steepness in terrain**
- **Snow or ice** conditions;
- Surface or **subsurface conditions** such as bare spots, forest growth, rocks, stumps
- Collision with **fixed structures** (e.g., lift towers and their components)
- Collisions with **other skiers**, and
- **Failure to ski or jump within the skier's own ability**

Utah State Law - Amended by Chapter 86, 1993 General Session

Inherent Risks of <u>Project Management</u>
Definitions

"Inherent risks of Project Management" means those dangers or conditions which are an integral part of project management including, but not limited to:

- Changing **client** conditions (which way the wind is blowing)
- Variations in **intensity** of client expectations
- Client or other stakeholder **coolness or frigidity**
- **Subsurface conditions** (e.g., rice bowls, client culture)
- Collision with **fixed structures** (e.g., closed organizations and minds)
- Collisions with **other Project Managers**
- **Failure to manage within your Project Management ability**

Probably a good idea. – Should be enacted.

==

What tips have you learned from the slopes?

==

Tough Project

Your Toughest Project

Sharing Our Project Stories

We were gathered at a corporate retreat in sessions where the facilitator was getting us to share stories about our projects. After each person told his or her story, we would discuss the aspects of the project that had made it easier or harder to

succeed. In one session, she asked us to talk about our toughest project. She had three volunteers.

Susan offered to tell us about one of her projects where she had to produce a new product on an extremely short schedule, much shorter than that for any similar work that they had done before.

Will offered to tell us about one of his projects where his client had only a vague idea of what he wanted, could not express it very well but, nevertheless, needed to have a perfect result.

Adele said she was sure she had a project that was tougher than either of the others. She was willing to bet that we would all agree that hers had been the toughest.

Susan's Story -- A Very Rapid Development

Background

Susan told us that her project required development of a special communication device for a very important client. The project was typical in content and complexity to other projects routinely performed by her organization and its contractor teammates. The average duration for such projects had been on the order of two to three years. However, this project had an exceptionally high priority and, because of a limited window of opportunity to get the product into service, the product had to be ***developed, tested, and delivered in only four months.*** If the product was not ready by then, the opportunity to use it would have passed and the product would have no other use.

Susan's Story

Shortly after lunch on Tuesday, the Division Director called me into his office and described the opportunity. He asked me if I could quickly put together a team and get the work done in four months. I said, "Give me two days and I'll get back to you to tell you what it will take to do it and how we would plan to go about it. Then, if you like our approach and can really commit the resources to do it – and guarantee no interruptions -- we'll get it done!"

I called three of my most trusted colleagues and two support contractor managers (one for hardware and one for software) and asked them to join me for a planning meeting. I also asked the client's "champion" of the project to come. I warned them all that if this meeting was successful they could all count on being committed to the job full-time for the next four months.

The next morning, I reviewed the problem. I presented my understanding of the user's concept of how and where the new device would be used and the deadlines we would have to meet to be successful. Then, we discussed the specific functions the product would need to perform, and the level of performance required for the situation. The client champion agreed with the description and said he would do whatever was necessary to help meet the shorter schedule.

We then discussed our ideas of how the key hardware and software components and some of the packaging concepts from their other products might be combined to provide a system with the required features and performance. We concluded that we could make that approach work. WE could follow a rapid prototyping process with the intention of fielding the final prototype.

After we agreed on the technical approach, I reminded everyone that We are going to have to do this *really fast*. Whatever we deliver will still have to be built with the same rigor as all our products. And, we will have to find ways of testing faster, too.

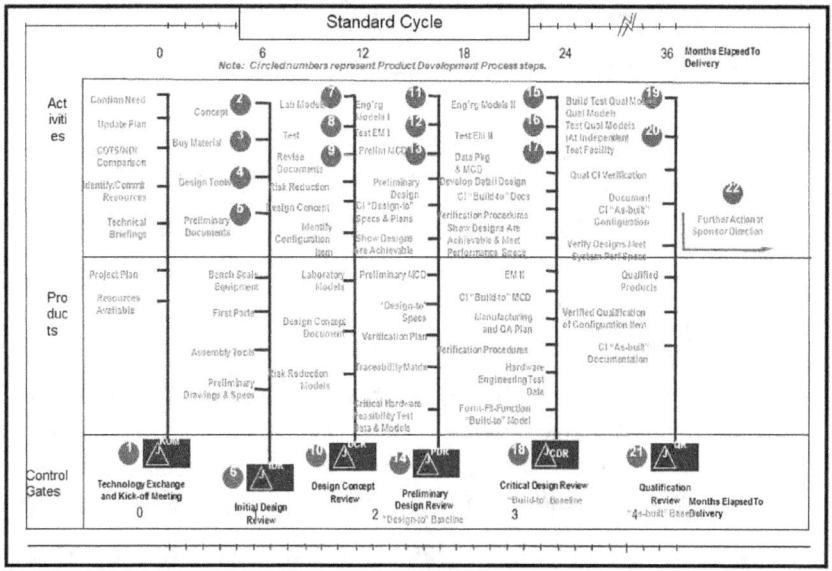

Four Months instead of Two Years

Then, I brought out a copy of the "Standard" process cycle chart and made some comments about the usual practices. I made these comments about the process shown in the chart.

- The typical process takes a couple of years. We have to do this in four months.
- The process in the chart was designed for "BIG" – *we're "small"*
- The chart's process was designed for a large, complex team – *we'll have only a few (probably 6 FT, 2 PT, 3 S/I plus the assigned staff from the two contractor organizations)*
- The chart's process was designed for substantial, intensive management oversight – *our managers want to stay informed, but they don't want to get in our way.*
- The chart was designed for a distributed team – *we can be <u>virtually</u> collocated: our contractor is only 1 ½ hours away by air and flights are frequent; we are tightly linked by secure phone and fax; and we've all worked together before.*

I then asked the group for their ideas on how best to satisfy the intent of the process but still complete the job in the four months allowed. I put these questions up on the whiteboard:

91

How can we safely shorten our schedule, given these facts?

- Technical review meetings normally take 2 days with 3 weeks preparation
- Documentation preparation takes too long
- Management reviews normally take two weeks

What are the major risks we are facing and what can we do to mitigate them?

- Interruptions by other projects
- Technical mis-steps (For example: Our hardware contractor's senior engineer really wants us to try his pet, new design for one of the key components. He claims it will work much better, but he hasn't proven it yet. How should we deal with that?)
- Mis-communication (different locations/different groups)

How should we go about tracking our cost, schedule, and technical progress?

- The standard systems are set up for a longer time frame. How can we shorten that?
- We have to "see" progress six times faster than normal. How can we do that?

What have I forgotten to tell you or to ask?

================= What Happened Then ===========

Commitment

Then, we worked out ways to deal with the problems and developed a new schedule. We got a firm commitment for the people we needed and got them dedicated at least 95% of their time. My boss helped enforce that by not pulling anyone out for any interruptions and by telling everyone else to "Get out of our way!"

We had 2 senior techies, a dedicated Ops guy, and a small, dedicated software contractor group. Our hardware contractor showed up with a similarly dedicated team of nine. There were no delays because someone was "busy on something else." We all knew our part of the business and we were tree and open in sharing our individual knowledge.

Rapid Reviews

To shorten the typical schedule, we pared down all the documents. Everyone kept good notes. We shared our notes electronically and used them as the basis for our brief, face-to-face or telephone reviews of each other's work. We lived on the secure telephone and fax and exchanged files over secure links. We "advanced" our reviews by phone and fax. The reviews took, at most, a couple of hours and we had all the key stakeholders present in person or by phone. We did one review, the CDR, in the classic manner to keep management happy.

Our client was a full-time member of the team, so we cut out the two-week review times for all the user reviews. He did his reviews by real-time participation in the team activities. His reviews took minutes or hours, not days or weeks.

Communication

When we had to, we hopped on a plane and went to the contractor site, reviewed what we needed to review and came back home the same day. No time wasted in motels or airports. We traveled as a group (sometimes the whole group would go to the contractor site for a one-day review) and that helped the team building.

Re-Use

We maximized the use of existing hardware, software and packaging ideas. Most of the items had been tested and qualified in a range that was appropriate for our target environment, so we could use them. That saved some component testing time, but we still had to do integration testing on everything. We planned that early so there would be no delays from not having things ready for integration when testing had to begin.

Risk Mitigation

The hardware contractor's Senior Engineer did get off in a different direction. He was on a quest to do something "nifty" with the technology and that would have slowed us down. It was risky because it was all new and couldn't be tested in time. We discovered that about a month and a half into the project and started another "risk mitigation design" that was sure to be ready in time. For a variety of reasons, the contractor let his Senior Engineer continue to work on his idea (but effectively took him out of the project) and we shifted to reliance on the version that we were sure would work.

Time Management

We developed our own cost, schedule, and technical performance control systems. Everyone kept track of their time and progress. We collected that information every week and re-planned as soon as we were sure where we were on all aspects.

Planning

The planning session at the beginning was really important. We had the whole team do a Cards-on-the-Wall exercise at the hardware contractor site right at the beginning. We got everyone to commit to their tasks and schedules and we held them to the commitments. When things changed (i.e., the Sr. Engineer issue) we went back to the wall and re-figured. The work plan was not a big document, it was a chart on the whiteboard right there on the wall for all to see.

How it Ended

My team followed the schedule and made the delivery on time in only four months. It was a tough job! It went really well! ...and now you know why.

At the beginning, my Division Chief said, 'I bet you can do it!', and he was right. It was really tough, but we did it!

================================

Will's Story: Managing with an "I'll know it when I see it". Client.

Background

Will said that a few years ago he had the privilege of being selected to be the project manager of a project to refurbish and re-equip the Assembly Chamber in the New York State Capitol building in Albany, New York. The job included many technical, political, and artistic challenges.

The Place

Known as the "People's Chamber," the home of the New York State Assembly is an historic architectural treasure. Designed in a Moorish-Gothic style – a trademark of its renowned American architect, Leopold Eidlitz, it was dedicated on January 1, 1879 to national acclaim. It is the largest room in the New York State Capitol, the first of the distinctive building's "Grand Spaces". In 1888, it was the first public room in the capitol and the first in the nation to be lit with electric lights.

The Project Team

Our contractor team included 11 different specialties, (e.g., construction, lighting, sound, interior design). Their job was to design, build and install new state-of-the-art lighting, sound reinforcement, paging, and electronic voting systems. Along with that, it required replacing the chamber carpet and cleaning and refurbishing all visible features including decorative stone friezes and statuary.

The work began the day after the end of the Assembly session at the end of March and had to be finished completely by the following January 4th when the governor would be coming to the Assembly to present the traditional State-of-the-State address. The deadline was absolute. Missing the deadline was politically unacceptable. Everything had to go right the first time.

Counsel for the Majority – The Top Decision-Maker

The person in charge of the project was a lawyer whose official title was Counsel to the Majority. He was the chief decision-maker and he held the purse strings for the job. He had no background in engineering or construction or any of the other specialties involved in the work. However, he was  politically sensitive and concerned about appearances – how the chamber and its new equipment would look when we finished.

The Counsel's charge to our contractor team was three-fold:

- Finish on time
- Make sure everything works
- Make it look great!

We assured him that we knew how to guarantee that we would finish on time and that everything would work. However, when we asked him for guidelines on "Looking Great", he said, "I'll know it when I see it" (This so-called **design guideline** is usually referred to by just the initial letters of the words, IKIWISI).

Tinkering to the Design

At the beginning, there was no detailed design or specification for the work. There was a list of all the things that had to be upgraded but none had been designed or specified. The contactors were all very knowledgeable about the kinds of items that would be needed, some of which (i.e., special lighting fixtures) would have to be specially fabricated. we concluded that we would have to take a tinkering approach to help the Counsel figure out what he wanted. Here's how we made that work.

Because of the Counsel's intense interest in the appearance of the final product, we agreed on a very careful step by step approach. As we conceived and designed new equipment and installations, we would first do a sketch to show the general idea. After the Counsel agreed to that, we would have an artist draw a picture of what it would look like when installed. If the Counsel liked that, we would go to the next step and build a physical mock-up of the item. Then, after approval by the Counsel, we would produce and install the final product. In each of these steps we tried to make sure that what we were showing was as close as possible to the final in appearance. At each stage of the tinkering, (i.e., rendering, mock-up, final) we would tinker with the details until the Counsel "Saw It" and gave us the go-ahead. The process worked well. Sometimes, we would have to tinker a lot with the renderings or models but the end product, a fully satisfied client, was worth the extra effort.

Some Examples

The first thing was the voting display system. We made up a picture of what it might look like and photoshopped the picture into a picture of the wall. He liked that.

| Voting Display Mock Up | Display Rendering | Final Version |

We did a similar series for the desk top box. That had to have a microphone, speaker, call buttons and voting buttons. There would be one on every one of the 144 desks. Here are examples of the designs at each stage of design of the desk top communications station.

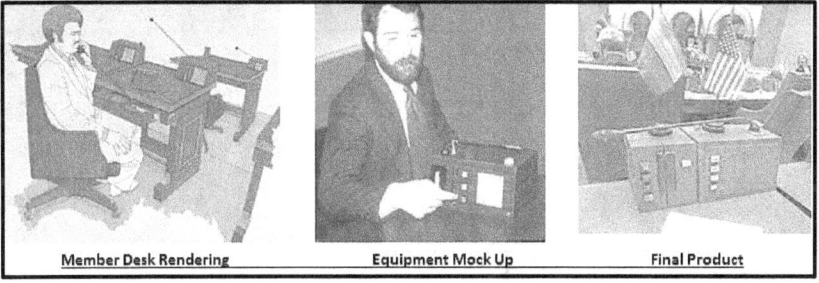

| Member Desk Rendering | Equipment Mock Up | Final Product |

We had all the contractor leads meet at the end of each day to review the sketches and drawings and resolve any conflicts or lingering design and construction issues. Then we would set the course for the next day. That ensured that there would be no free-lance tinkering by any of the 11 contractors and we would end up with exactly what was agreed to by the Counsel.

Our approach to dealing with an IKIWISI client is called WYSIWYG (What You See Is What You Get). It ensured no missteps or delays in the project.

Keeping Notes

Several of the contractors carried and used their cameras to capture pictures of problems and progress on their parts of the project. Review of the photos was on the agenda for every morning team meeting. Selected photos were used in meetings with the Counsel --- mainly to remind him of what he had seen and agreed to.

Photos helped see the unseen. The camera saw it all. The team members all had many distractions while working but the cameras did not. The cameras saw everything and remembered it. Here is a photo from mid-December as we  were starting to put things together.

Taking photos from the same spots each day allowed the team to see the rate of progress of the demolition and construction in a time-lapse view. They could see what they were getting done.

At the beginning, we set aside an extra amount for all the design work. That was an extra 25% above what the work would have cost if we had had good specs and designs at the outset. It turned out that that was enough – the Counsel was easy to work with.

At the end of the project, the renderings, models and the photos were retained in the project notebooks. Those records documented the tinkering path of the design team. The combination of renderings, models and photos was critical in helping the client and the team see how the requirements were evolving.

How it Ended

Will was happy to tell us that, despite all the problems, his team:

- Finished On-Time
- Finished On-Budget, and
- The final product not only looked great but got rave reviews in the press.

He reminded all of us to beware of a client whose project specification is 'I'll know it when I see it." That project is likely to be your "Toughest Project."

==================================

Adele's Story: Managing a Relocation

Background

Adele told us her toughest project was to plan and execute the relocation of an old organization that had been operating in one place for a long time. Over the last several years this organization had found the need to rely on additional staff to provide an ever-increasing number of special support services from many different sources. It had become clear that the need for these services is likely to continue to grow substantially in diversity and intensity.

It had also become very clear that the expense and coordination of the many, required services was too burdensome now and would only increase in the future at this location. The organization needed to move to a new location where the required services could be obtained in a better coordinated and less expensive way. There were many options available for making this transition.

Adele said her project was to select the best option for the future location and manage all aspects of the transition from the old to the new environment.

What could be hard about that?

The "Organization"

Adele went on to say that If this had been a normal business organization, it could have been a pretty straightforward job. However, this one was different. The "organization" was a couple of senior citizens who had reached a point where they needed to make a big change in their lives. They and their close family members had determined that they were physically, financially, and socially at risk in their current home. They needed to move into a situation that could comprehensively and consistently provide the support they will need as they continue to age. As project manager, Adele said, I had to start by finding suitable new options and helping those two seniors agree to and commit to the move.

100

After that, she said, my activities focused on preserving things that they would need in the new environment, disposing of everything they wouldn't need (including their current house or apartment), repackaging their lives to fit the new situation, getting them there in good shape and helping them settle in and thrive in their new environment. If that sounds like an easy project, it isn't. There are many aspects that combine to make it really tough.

No Top Level Support

Adele told us about an old cartoon strip in which a Boy Scout, eager to do a good deed, insisted on helping an old lady go across the street. They made it across the street safely. Then, she thanked him and asked to go back --*because she really didn't want to go in the first place*.

Adele said, I told that story to highlight the fact that the main subjects of my project, the seniors I was trying to help by getting them into a better environment, really did not want to go. They clung to an outdated vision of going to *The Old Folks Home*, a nursing facility where residents receive food and shelter and lead a limited life until they die.

She noted that today, there are many new options for active seniors to get the additional support they need as they become less able to deal with the various aspects of their lives. The feared "Home" has now been replaced by a continuum of choices. I had to do a lot of homework to determine the most acceptable new home.

She continued. I had to obtain a good assessment and forecast of my seniors' needs. Then, I had to gather information on the possible choices (e.g., services provided, location, affordability, facilities). After that, I had to present them to the seniors, overcome their misconceptions about the options and help them arrive at a decision on when and where to relocate. This was hard to achieve but it was a critical first step.

What made this particularly hard was the fact that there were so many other stakeholders involved. Their children had strong feelings also – some in favor of making the move and some against. Emotions ran high. There were issues with where the seniors should go (i.e., who should they be near?), what should happen to their current home, what should be done with the items they could not take with them, and so on. The differences among all the participants were more complex than Middle East peace talks. I had to find a way to achieve consensus with everyone equally dis-satisfied (or satisfied) with the final result.

Uncertainties and Risks

If there had been no uncertainty or risks this project would have been easier for me, she said. However, this project involved uncertainties and risks in real estate and investment values, and the health of the principal subjects.

Financial Uncertainties

Housing: The new situation had to be affordable. What will the new home cost? How will they pay for it? What will their house sell for? Will they have some equity to use to help them purchase or rent their new abode? Will they make or lose money on the sale? Will they need to dip into savings to afford the new place?

Living Expenses: The clients needed assurance of some consistent regular income (e.g., Social Security, pensions). They also had other investments and IRAs that could be tapped for living expenses. The values of these varies and was a source of uncertainty.

Some expenses they now have would be going away (e.g., home maintenance, lawn care)? What expense are likely to be less (e.g., real estate tax, home owner's insurance, utilities)? What expenses will stay the same or possibly be greater (e.g., condo fees, meal plans)?

I had to nail down all of these current and future financial questions about capital and operating expenses before I could address the next question – Will they be able to afford to continue at the new location despite normal fluctuations of the economy?

What will happen to their investments? Will the results of their home sale add to or subtract from their retirement investment pool? What income can they expect to get from Social Security, IRAs, pensions, and other investments through good times and bad?

Performance Uncertainty: More questions for me to resolve:

We had long discussions about whether the new situation would be satisfactory and provide all the needed services? Would their health hold up through the moving process? Would they need to have additional help or transportation assistance? Could there be a risk of surprise costs (e.g., special assessments, staff annual tips). How will these affect their financial and psychological situation?

Clear, Stable Requirements

As I progressed through the project, I was threading my way through a minefield of rules. The rules shape the requirements. Everybody had rules and they often conflicted with each other. Retirement communities have rules on how old one has to be and how physically able and well people must be to enter. Each state has rules about retirement community operations and care. Real estate rules cover the sale of the home.

Disposal Rules

Studies have shown that the typical home contains more than 10,000 items and there are rules for every type of item. My seniors had at least that many items. While disposing of them

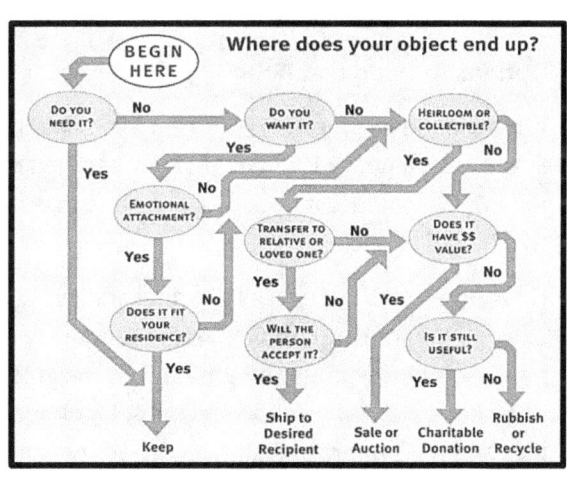

during downsizing we found that consignment shops, donation organizations and even trash disposal organizations all have their own rules. Some would come and pick up donations if they are left outside. Some required us to drop off the items during certain times. Some would come into the home to remove larger items and some would not.

(Note: Downsizing chart, © Garaceful Transitions.com – with permission)

One special case for us included some highly prized items that contained prohibited materials (e.g., ivory carvings, eagle feathers). We found a museum for them.

No Time to Do Careful Planning

With all those uncertainties, requirements had to be updated every day and re-planning was a constant. The pace of action on this project was fast. Everything changed every day and there was constant pressure to re-act to crises here and now rather than to take time to anticipate potential problems and plan to deal with them in an orderly way.

An Achievable Schedule

It looked easy at first. Find the new environment and secure it. But, we had many schedule unknowns. When would the new place be available? There was a waiting list, and a suitable apartment or condo was not immediately available until someone relocated (e.g., moved away or died). When would our seniors take up residence and/or start paying for it? When would the old home sell? How would we handle any gaps in timing? How long would it take to set up bridge financing?

Options to Undo and ReDo

What's done is done! This phrase hasn't changed one bit since Shakespeare wrote it down. It still means exactly what Lady Macbeth meant. We could not change the past, so we did not dwell on it. There was no going back.

House sales and purchases are final and could only be reversed at great expense of time and money. Items sent away during downsizing were gone, sold or donated and are not recoverable. Household goods that had been retained (*maybe too many*) had been moved into the new digs and my seniors have moved in. So, now it was time to move forward and think about what to do next instead of focusing on what's already happened.

But, there was still one more part – perhaps the toughest part of the project.

Closing Out the Project - Notifications

My seniors had a lot of organizations and people to notify – more than they knew – and they did not have very good records. Some of the organizations they dealt with had changed in the last few years from paper records to electronic systems – with passwords – and who remembered them? No one!

For each, we had to know the currently recorded information, the way to make the change, (e.g., by phone, e-mail, letter) and, if necessary, have the passwords or personal identification available to tell the organization that you are authorized to make the change. (I said this was really tough.)

In the notification process, we were rarely dealing with real people. We were dealing with phone robots, widely varying web sites and arcane government forms. Each will require different information. Some of the attempted notifications failed and we found out about this months later by continuing to see bills for services thought to be concluded and by seeing mail that has been forwarded to the old address. This was a case where what was done **was not done** and it had to be done again, and again, until it stopped.

Utilities	Financial & Personal Accounts	Government	Services
☐ Electric	☐ Banks	☐ Post Office	☐ Attorney
☐ Gas/Oil	☐ Credit Agencies	☐ Government &	☐ Pool Services
☐ Water	(Experian, etc)	Public Offices	☐ Lawn/Garden
☐ Garbage/Trash	☐ Loan Institutions	☐ Veteran Affairs	Services
☐ Telephone -Landline	☐ Credit Card	☐ Income Tax: Federal	☐ Housecleaner
☐ Telephone – Mobile	Companies	State	Physicians
☐ Cable	☐ Department Stores	☐ Family Support	☐ Veterinarians
☐ Internet	☐ Insurance Agencies	☐ Social Security	☐ Accountant/Tax
☐ Water Delivery	☐ Pension Plan	☐ Motor Vehicle Car	Consultant
	☐ Rewards Programs	and Driver	**On-Line Accounts**
Subscriptions	☐ Professional	Registration	☐ AAA
☐ Newspapers	Associations	☐ Voter Registration	☐ AARP
☐ Magazines		☐ Social Security	☐ Amazon
☐ Mail Order Catalogs		☐ Pension Benefits	☐ Apple
☐ Book Clubs		Administrator	☐ Google
			☐ Microsoft

What Makes a Project Easy?

Adele finished by reminding us of the things we had all learned through the years about what makes a project easy?

- Top level involvement and support,
- Few uncertainties and risks
- Clear, stable requirements,
- Time to do careful planning
- An achievable schedule
- Options to recover (i.e., UnDo or ReDo) when you make a mistake.

See, it Was Really Tough!

Adele claimed that none of the easy factors were there for her project. The seniors didn't really want to go. The children had a lot of conflicting ideas. So much for management support. The number of uncertainties and risks was mind-boggling. There were surprises every day and it was hard to set aside enough reserve to mitigate them.

She said she had to spend many hours, adjusting the requirements to avoid the hidden dangers in the rules minefield. With so many balls in the air at one time her planning had to be done on the fly. Her overall schedule was dominated by others, (e.g., realtors, sales people, movers) and their schedules usually conflicted. She had to live with her mistakes and their consequences with no do-overs.

How it Turned Out

When she finished, Adele told us that the relocation had been completed and she hoped that her seniors were enjoying their new situation. Then, she asked the others in the group if they agreed with her that her project was the toughest. They all agreed and were concerned that someday in the future they would get that same kind of project ---and it was good to be forewarned.

==================================

===================================

Advice from an Expert

Theodore "Rough Rider" Roosevelt was famous for taking on and successfully completing tough projects (e.g., finishing the Panama Canal, exploring the River of Doubt). His advice to those who take on tough projects is **"Do what you can, with what you have, where you are."**

If you agree to accept the offer to manage **"The Toughest Project"**, you should heed Teddy's advice. Work hard, be aware, be flexible and be ready to deal with the situation as it evolves.

===================================

RMS Titanic

Prepare for Titanic Problems

Problems Don't Add Up: They Multiply

You remember Murphy's Law, "If anything can go wrong, it will." That's why you do risk analysis for your projects. You also need to remember the crucial addition to Murphy's Law: "... and it will go wrong at the worst time." The worst time is when you already have other problems occurring at the same time.

The Titanic

We know the tragic result of the Titanic's collision with the iceberg. We also know that the loss of the ship and the great loss of life came about because several problems occurred at the same time, each one reinforcing and magnifying the others. The lookouts did not have binoculars (left behind when they sailed). The radio operators did not get the messages about the icebergs. One too many of the "watertight" compartments failed and, although there were lifeboats, there were too few and no one knew how to deploy them effectively. Later studies have identified 13 simultaneous problems, each one exacerbating the initial one. Take any one of those out of the equation and the results would likely have been much less tragic.

> ### Score ‖   Problems ... 13+
> ### ‖   Titanic 0

Your Titanic Situations

As a good project manager, you of course have a risk plan for your project and you have all the potential problems you have foreseen individually listed and arranged by probability and impact. However, have you ever considered situations where several of those problems might occur at the same time? Think about the examples below.

Example # 1 – Snow-Mageddon

Look at what some folks in New England faced in the winter of 2015. It snowed every few days for over a month. The Boston area had over eight feet of snow and freezing temperatures throughout February. Try to imagine running your business in this situation.

If you worked in New England, you would know there is a risk that, with a heavy snowfall, your staff members might not be able to get to the office (#1) so you set up procedures for staying linked by telecommuting. However, what if the power to your building also goes out for several days? No one can link to your office network (#2). To top it off, imagine if two key employees were hospitalized with storm-related problems. One has a heart attack shoveling snow (#3) and the other falls while clearing snow off the roof of his home and is badly injured (#4).

Score ‖   **Problems ... 4**
  ‖   **Business 0**

Welcome to today's world of simultaneous multiple problems.

Example # 2 – Multiple Operations Problems

Say you work in a company that uses very specialized equipment to produce unusual products (e.g., fine art graphics materials). Your equipment uses volatile inks and specialized paper. Yours is a safety-minded company and you know that there is a constant risk of fire, so you have regular fire drills. Those are always scheduled for nice days – but what if it was real fire (#1) on a day with horrible weather outside and your staff is not allowed back in the building for an extended period (#2). You have two problems at the same time – a fire and your employees are exposed to bad weather. Each one is bad by itself. Together, they are much worse.

However, let's add one more problem. Let's say that the fire was in your graphics section and it destroyed your specialized printers (#3). Your risk plan covered that. You know that those can be replaced quickly by a local supplier and you have a good relationship with her. So, you call her and tell her you need the replacements NOW! But, she's out of stock (#4) and has some on the way but they are on a ship in Long Beach that is not being unloaded because of a dockworkers' strike (# 5).

Now let's really pile it on. There are no local systems that can work with your backup graphics data (#6) to continue your project. You will have to farm it out to the only other firm that does the same kind of thing and they are in France. We'll leave it there but a lot more could happen.

Score ‖	Problems ….. 6
‖	Business……. 0

Don't think this is possible? Think about something that has gone wrong recently and see how many different problems were involved in making it worse than it could have been.

Example # 3 – Multiple Schedule Problems

Fred Brooks said in The Mythical Man Month: "Projects get late one day at a time." Here is a personal experience of how it happened to me. Your project could have the same type of schedule delay.

My refrigerator quit working on Tuesday. Being prepared for that problem (#1), I called the local appliance store and the dealer said that he would get one out to me tomorrow. A replacement was delivered on Wednesday afternoon. I was not prepared for the second problem. On Thursday afternoon, the replacement refrigerator was still warm inside (#2). I called the dealer and he said he would send another replacement as soon as he could, but he had no more in the store (#3) and would have to get it from his wholesaler. He called the wholesaler who said that he would normally ship it on Monday, but Monday was a national holiday (#4) so it would not get to the dealer until Tuesday afternoon and to me on Wednesday – eight days after my original refrigerator broke down.

Score ‖	Problems ….. 4
‖	Consumer …. 0

Fortunately, the weather was good, the roads were clear, and the delivery guys showed up for work, the truck didn't break down and the refrigerator came, and it worked. Otherwise the problem score could have been higher. Multiple problems turned what should have been a one-day replacement into a week-and-a-day process. What if this wasn't just a homeowner's issue? What if I ran a restaurant and I didn't have a refrigerator for eight days? My business might never have recovered from this disaster.

Planning for Multiple Risks

Could multiple problems happen to you and your business? The next time you sit down to discuss your risk list, take a moment to think about the possible combinations and how those might multiply the potential impact. Plan your projects and your business so that you are prepared, not just for a single problem, but for a number of separate problems that could magnify the loss – and even sink your ship.

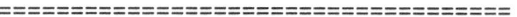

BiZ-Risk: A Team Game

A Team Game to Help Manage Risk

You and your project team are probably pretty good at identifying the risks that you are likely to encounter. If you have some real pessimists on your team you may find that they can think up even the most unlikely risks you could face. Getting a comprehensive list of the risks and evaluating their probability and impact on your project is good. Unfortunately, many project teams stop there. They prepare their ranked list of risks and then try to prevent their occurrence. They are not always successful. What they feared actually happens. So, then what should they do?

When one of the risks actually materializes it becomes an issue that now must be actively managed. That's a whole new problem — one that has different dynamics and requires different skill sets. The time for prevention is over. Now the team has to work its way through a crisis.

In a Harvard Business Review article, Norm Augustine recommended what you need to do to "Manage the Crisis You Tried to Prevent." They are:

1. **Recognize the problem**
2. **Prepare to manage the new crisis**
3. **Determine how to resolve the problems**
4. **Organize to manage the problem**
5. **Develop a containment strategy — and use it**
6. **Plan future prevention**
7. **Close out the effort when you are done**

This is good advice from a recognized expert in the field. Maybe your team has already thought through all of these potential steps for all of the risks they have forecast. If they have, that would be very unusual. Most teams do not start to think about these things until the moment the risk appears on their doorstep ready to be managed. That's too late and that's why we have invented this game.

BiZ-Risk: The Game

This game is designed for project work teams to play from time-to-time, perhaps at a "Brown-Bag Lunch." The primary purpose of the game is to get the team thinking about the situations that Norm has suggested. It is also intended to be interesting, instructive, useful, and FUN!

How to Play BiZ-Risk

The players should include members of the project team or work group that share the same set of risks. Many of them will probably have participated earlier in development of the group's Risk list. Any number can play but it's best to have at least three. To start, each player should choose a number between 1 and 7. This will determine their order of play. The game is played by having players address the key questions that Augustine's article suggested.

Scoring

Players score points by coming up with good answers for their assigned questions. Scoring is as follows:

- Provide the initial answer to a question: 4 Points
- Add significantly to an initial answer: 1 Point
- Leader may award extra points for exceptional contribution to an answer.
- Players should try to accumulate as many points as possible.

One person should be chosen to lead the game, keep score, and, at the end, to summarize the results. The game starts with the leader choosing a risk at random from the group's documented Risk List. That risk, identified earlier, will be subject of all further play.

Play starts with Player # 1 addressing Question # 1.

After the player provides an answer the group will discuss the answer until they reach agreement. Players gain points based on the outcome of the discussion. (See scoring rules, above.)

Play proceeds with the next player addressing the next question.

The Questions

1. Recognize the Problem: How can we tell if this is really the risk we identified earlier or something else?

2. Prepare to Manage the Issue: How could we determine how big a deal this is going to be for us?

3. Resolve the Problems: What will we have to do to resolve the issue?

4. Organize to Manage the problem: How could we organize our team to manage this?

5. Develop a Containment Strategy: How can we best limit the damage?

6. Plan Future Prevention: How could this have been prevented?

7. Close Out the Effort: How would we know when we are done?

Play ends after the last player answers the last question. At that point the leader summarizes the results of the discussions and totals the scores.

Here is an Example:

An active project team had these three items on their Risk Watch List. They start with Risk # 1.

1. Project estimates may turn out to be much too low: Estimates may be unrealistically too low and may jeopardize our cost and schedule performance ratings with our client.

2. Process inputs are low quality: Inputs from stakeholders may be too low quality to be actionable (e.g. poorly written business case, unclear change requests).

3. Recognize the Problem: How can we tell if this is really the risk we identified earlier or something else?

Jane started by addressing the first question: *How can we tell if this is really the risk we identified earlier or something else?*

Jane: I think the first thing we need to do is go over the assumptions the estimators made about how much work was really involved. We should see if they had a complete Work Breakdown Structure and check it to see if their estimates for this type of work were based on experience or were just guesses. **(4 points for being first)**

Chris: We better also check to be really sure that execution is not also part of the mis-match problem. We could really be taking longer than we should for some parts of the work. **(1 point for adding comment)**

Charlie took on the second question: **How could we determine how big a deal this is going to be for us?**

Charlie: We are probably going to have to take some time and go over the estimate process very carefully. As Jane said, we need to look at the WBS they were working with and redo it if necessary. **(4 Points)**
Roger: They had some people they called "experts" making guesses on some of the weird stuff so we better check just how "expert" they really were. **(1 Point)**

Adjuan addressed #3: **What will we have to do to resolve the issue?**

Adjuan: There are several things to be resolved. First, the estimates have to be corrected. Then, we have got to get the work we're doing lined up with the estimates. Finally, we've got to get our client on board with what we're doing. **(4 Points)**
Chris: I'll go back to my earlier comment. We had better be certain that we are not really taking too long to do our tasks. We should review what we have done so far to be sure. **(1 Point)**

Natasha spoke about organizing: **How could we organize our team to manage this?**

Natasha: There is enough of a problem here that we would need to set up a mini project within our team to address it. We could task that project to: correct the estimate and the estimating process; adjust the cost and schedule targets; and re-align the project tasking. **(4 Points)**.
Sonja: We would also need to set a near term target date to get all this done so we won't have a continuing crisis. **(1 Point)**

Roger started with #5: **How can we best limit the damage?**

Roger: We have to openly acknowledge that we have this problem and let all the shareholders know that we are busy working on it. This is not only a technical problem, it has a Public Relations component, too.

Natasha: There may be some contract issues here. Someone will need to check that. **(1 Point)**

Sonja: This kind of thing could easily happen again, so we had better document these ideas and put them in our Risk Lessons Learned file. **(1 Point)**

Sonja answered #6: **How could this have been prevented?**

Sonja: We should have picked up this problem sooner. We should have been able to see the discrepancy after just a couple of weeks. **(4 Points)**
Chris: We should tighten up our process to compare the progress of the project against the estimates. **(1 Point)**

Adjuan: We could have gotten together as a team at the beginning and worked through the estimate with the estimators. **(1 Point)**

Chris took on # 7: **How would we know when we are done?**

Chris: I'm not sure that we will ever be completely done with this issue. Requirements keep changing so we are always going to have to keep making new estimates and checking them. We'll be done when we have confidence that our estimating process is working well, and the estimates and actuals are consistently in sync. **(4 Points)**

> **End of the Example – Scores**
> Jane   4 + 0
> Charlie   4 + 0
> Adjuan   4 + 1
> Natasha 4 + 1
> Roger   4 + 1
> Sonja   4 + 2
> Chris   4 + 3

It's More than Just a Game
I am reminded of the story about a dog who liked to chase sports cars. He always believed that there was a good probability that he might catch one. Then, one day he did catch one — and he had no idea what to do with it. So, it is with most project teams that I have worked with. They know that there is a probability of many different bad things that

could happen, but they don't really have much of an idea about what to do about them when they occur.

We could have presented this concept as a checklist for "What to Do When the Risk Comes True" but that would have made it look like a chore. The game approach should be more fun and has the potential to yield some other benefits.

First, it includes all of the key questions that need to be addressed in these situations. Second, it provides practice for the team members in thinking about and sharing ideas about a critical aspect of their work. Finally, if it just so happens that the team chooses to play a risk that really does become an issue on their project they are way ahead of the game. BiZ-Risk Game will have prepared them for the real business game.

==

Ready to play? It's your turn.

==

Section 5 - Final Stories

The final two stories work as a pair. The first one presents the increasing challenges faced by project managers and teams in this ever more complex world. The second offers advice on how to inspire project teams to work hard to achieve success in the face of those challenges.

95% is Not a Passing Grade

This is an old story that becomes more relevant every day. In it, soon to be graduates from high school are given a dose of real-world advice about the performance challenges they will face as they enter the world of work. The examples cited in the story clearly show how future success depends on top-level performance.

Poetic Project Management

To succeed as a project manager, you must not only make sure your team members are trained and instructed on the tasks to be done, you must also inspire them to do the work well. This story includes several examples in which outstanding managers crafted their words to inspire their teams and achieve excellent performance.

===

Preparation for Real Life

Ninety-five Percent is NOT a Passing Grade

Graduation Preparation

Graduation time was approaching, and the principal of the high school was speaking to an assembly program of seniors. His topic today was future grading systems. He told the seniors that they would likely find the grading system quite different after they left school and joined the world of work.

He reviewed the present grading scheme where 95-100 = A, and 85-94 = B, and 75-84 = C.

Then, he pointed out that next year this was going to change for them. The new rules would be that anything less than 100% would be considered a failure. Only 100% would rate as "A" and there would be no other grades.

Then, he waited for a stunned silence followed by a lot of short, whispered exchanges. Inevitably, somebody would ask, "What do you mean? We won't be getting report cards after we get out of school, will we?"

Reality Sets In

That question, variously stated, provided the opening he wanted. He used it to lay out reality in terms that every one of those graduating seniors could clearly understand. He would point out that graduates turned workers would, indeed, be getting a report card every day. For example, if you were working as a secretary after graduation, you could not reply to your angry boss, "But I spelled 95% of the words in every letter correctly today." (After all, 95% in school is a passing grade in spelling.) If you were employed as a bookkeeper you could not say, "I got the correct balance 95% of the time today." Or, if you were working as a truck driver, you would probably not have to come to work tomorrow if you told your boss that you successfully avoided only 95% of all of the other vehicles on the road today.

The first two examples usually fired up the students' interest because they knew they would be doing things like this soon. Still, since they had not yet done these things they thought that they might be allowed a few honest errors. The driving example really hit hard though, because every one of them had already driven a car and realized full well that 100% was the minimum passing grade for driving.

Today's Report Card

Many years have gone by since I first heard that speech, but there has been no change in the grading scheme for post-school life and work. In fact, it has become more difficult and more important to achieve the top grade. Our highways are more crowded. Speeds are faster, reducing the tolerance for errors on the freeway. Our computer systems multiply human efforts a million-fold. Tiny errors in the design or programming can produce gigantic disasters. In our complex business systems, accumulations of small errors can lead to the buildup of major strains which can topple giant corporations and bend the economy to the breaking point.

Today' World

In the 'Readin, 'Ritin and 'Rithmetic of today's business, we have to demand grades of 100%. Anything less will be hard to accept. If your company's 24/7 computer system only scores 98 % (equal to an A minus) the system will be down 14 Hours, 24 Minutes each month. That's almost 29 minutes a day. Can you live with that?

If the airline reservation system you are calling scores a low A-minus (95%) it will not be available 5% of the time. Don't call during the day and a half each month that it's not available. And let's not talk about parachutes, scuba systems, surgery robots, collision avoidance systems and all the other inventions of the modern world. They all require the very top grade.

The goal of 100% is not an impossible dream. After all, it was always possible to get an "A" in school if we did all the work that was required and applied ourselves. But how many times did we really apply ourselves and how hard did we really try?

Process improvement programs that achieve zero defects (100% error-free) are achievable. Fail-safe systems that provide 100% up-time for vital services such as 911 are being built. These are being done by people who study the problems, learn about the techniques and tools, do their homework, and apply themselves to the tasks at hand. They are getting straight As.

===================================

What will be on your report card?

===================================

===================================

This article is based on a talk my father, the high school principal, gave to graduating seniors about to enter the working world. He considered this as his last chance to teach a vital lesson. His students have done well in later years and the lesson he taught them is even more appropriate today than it was then.

===================================

==

"Tell me the facts and I'll learn. Tell me the truth and I'll believe. But tell me a story and it will live in my heart forever."

Native American Proverb

==

Poetic Project Management

Manage Carefully, Speak Poetically

As a project manager, you employ structured thinking and creativity with **people** to create a desired result. Poets employ *structured thinking and creativity with **language** to create a desired result.* What could happen if you combined your skills ***with people and language,*** and became a Poetic Project Manager?

Sidney Harman, Harman Industries founder once said, *"I used to tell my senior staff to get me poets as managers. Poets are our original systems thinkers. They look at our most complex environments and they reduce the complexity to something they begin to understand."*

You Could Become a Poetic Project Manager

As a Poetic Project manager, you could be more effective. You would take extra care with your language as you lead your teams through the various phases of your projects. You would sharpen and convey to your team a more exciting vision of the end result of the project. You would choose the right words and arrange them in ways that would help you focus the team on important matters, clarify complex processes, and remind them of what is needed for success. As your project progresses, your well-chosen words, arranged with care, would help you motivate, inspire, and reward your team. You really should do it.

Here are some examples of how others have successfully practiced poetic project management.

==

A Poetic Vision for the Harley-Davidson V-Rod

By carefully crafting his words, a poetic project manager at Harley-Davidson evoked a very clear vision of the challenge for his team. He told his long-time Harley team members that they would be building the next generation Harley, better than all they had built before and more ***HARLEY*** than ever.

Here's How He Did It

At their project initiation meeting, the project manager at Harley-Davidson told the team, *"We will be doing something we have never done before. We will be building a new, liquid cooled, 115 horsepower cycle with an exposed steel and aluminum body."* That in itself was pretty exciting, but then he added a poetic touch:

> "It will embody the **American Spirit,**
>
> It will **Scream Harley.**
>
> When you hear it, it will say,
>
> ### *HARLEY!"*

==

Poetry to Provide Motivation

A former colleague, Hilary Findlay, told me about a person leading a group of avid mountain climbing hobbyists on a climb of Mount Kilimanjaro, the tallest in Africa. The person leading the group was not only an experienced project manager, he was a poetic one. As the story goes, here's how the leader described the adventure and motivated the climbers.

> We will struggle through the jungle,
> Emerging on grassy plains.
> Then we'll reach the foothills,
> And repack for the climb.
> And when we reach the summit
> ### All of Africa will be beneath our feet.

The final line poetically provided the team with the climbers' ultimate reward. They had done much more than just conquer a mountain – they had conquered a continent!

====================================

A Poetic Way to Focus Attention:

Clarence (Kelly) Johnson was the long-time manager of the Lockheed Skunk Works, a super- secret facility that developed advanced reconnaissance planes (e.g. U-2, SR-71) for the government. He had strong feelings about how the Skunk Works should operate and stated his 14 Rules for Project Management. Those rules provided the details of his management practices. They were clear, but wordy. So, to focus attention on the most critical aspects, he produced:

- **Be quick,**
- **Be quiet,**
- Be on time!
- .and **Keep It Simple, Stupid!** *(KISS)*

Those were the most important things for his team to keep in mind as they followed Kelly's rules.

==================================

Using Poetry to Clarify and Simplify a Process

It is hard to get project teams to adopt and use effective process improvement practices. There are many books about how to do it. Most of the books go in great detail about how to: (1) document a process; (2) ensure that it is followed and tracked; (3) examine the results to find flaws in the process; (4) ensure that the flaws are fixed and then; (5) keep doing those things continuously. A simpler way to explain all that is with a poem.

> *Draw what you do, Do what you draw*
> *Find and Fix every flaw.*
> *Track Performance to ensure*
> *You're on the path to be mature.*
> *(Repeat as necessary)*

The poem explains the fundamentals and is easier to remember than pages of instructions.

==================================

Poetry to Inspire Creativity

William Ayot, a British management presenter, poet and coach created this poem to inspire team members to free their minds from the hypnotism of routine and let themselves doodle.

> *Another meeting, another agenda, another list of buzz-words, initials and initiatives.*
>
> *The muse lies minimised in the corner of our screens*
>
> *Not dead, not buried, but ignored and unseen,*
>
> *Like a doodle at the edge of an action plan*
>
> *Me? I say make a sacrifice to doodle;*
>
> *Pick some flowers, speak a poem, feed the tiny muse*.
>
> From "A Doodle at the Edge" by William Ayot

Doodling is defined as "drawing absent-mindedly." However, evidence has shown that the mind is not absent, it is enjoying a bit of freedom, playing around with ideas, some of which it allows to escape through the doodling pencil where they can be seen in the light of day.

===================================

Poetry to Recognize and Reward

A famous Apple commercial by Rob Siltanen included a beautifully crafted free verse poem that recognized and praised the innovative people who were working at Apple.

"Here's to the crazy ones. The misfits. The rebels. The troublemakers. The round pegs in the square holes. The ones who see things differently. They're not fond of rules. And they have no respect for the status quo. You can quote them, disagree with them, glorify or vilify them. About the only thing you can't do is ignore them. Because they change things. They push the human race forward. And while some may see them as the crazy ones, we see genius. Because the people who are crazy enough to think they can change the world, are the ones who do."

That ad had a double purpose. It was intended not only to recognize and reward the innovators at Apple but also to change for the better the public image of the Hippie-like Apple employees. The continued fame of that ad is testimony to the lasting power of its poetry.

===================================

Poetry for Team Building

One poetic project manager decided to have a Haiku contest as a team building exercise. Haiku is a very structured form of poetry. It traditionally consists of 17 syllables in three lines of 5, 7, and 5 syllables, respectively. The project team consisted of a number of highly skilled programmers and engineers who thrived on complex tasks and the manager thought this would be both challenging and fun for all. The project manager asked the team to construct Haiku poems about their project. He showed them some samples.

> Deadlines are vital
> Keeping us all organized
> I should set some now

> Tasks running over
> Flustered people all around
> Time for Get Up, Go.

===

Final Message (from the Author)

Craft your messages, take the time

Use blank verse, free verse, haiku, rhyme

Arrange your words so they strike home

... Be more successful with a poem.

===================================

* The poem, **Draw What You Do**, is from the author's book with that name.

===================================

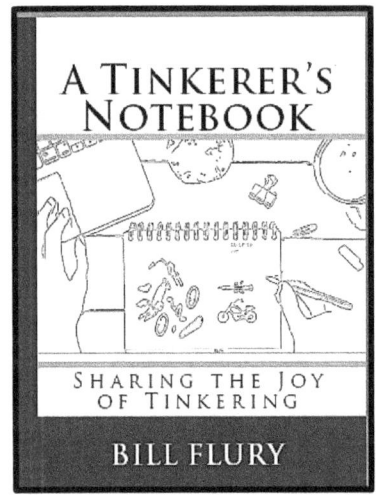

Other Books by Bill Flury

Draw What You Do: A Practical Approach to Process Improvement

ISBN-13: 9781494275181

ISBN-10: 149427518X

This book is about you and the things you do – the processes in which you are involved and the way you do them. If your processes at work or at home are beset with surprises, crises, delays, misunderstandings and other forms of headaches, "Relief is on the Way." This book shows some easy things you and your co-workers can do on your own to minimize mistakes, crises, and delays in the ways you interact.

WYSIWYG Tales: See and Improve What You Do

ISBN-13: 978-1494256975

ISBN-10: 1494256975

Here are stories about people who found ways to see and understand how things they do with others fit together – or not. Some found ways to solve their problems and avoid crises. Others learned how they could improve coordination with colleagues and friends and see beneficial things they could or should be doing

A Tinkerer's Notebook: Sharing the Joy of Tinkering

ISBN-13: 978-1539788508

ISBN-10: 1539788504

A lifetime tinkerer lets you see some pages from his notebook, so you can share the joy he finds in tinkering. His notes about his own tinkering tell how his family, friends and his environment encouraged and enabled him to tinker from his earliest days and onward through his working life. He describes the principles and practices that he and other tinkerers follow to ensure success.

Don't Blame Fred: Build Blame-Free Processes

ISBN-13: 978-1979178846

ISBN-10: 1979178844

Don't Blame Fred, is a collection of real-life stories about people who stopped blaming each other for their problems by discovering new and better ways to work together. The stories are drawn from the author's experience in successfully managing 85 challenging and widely varied projects. The stories all relate to situations that required thoughtful application of the standard practices described in the several different project management handbooks on his bookshelf.